EYEWITNESS
TITANIC

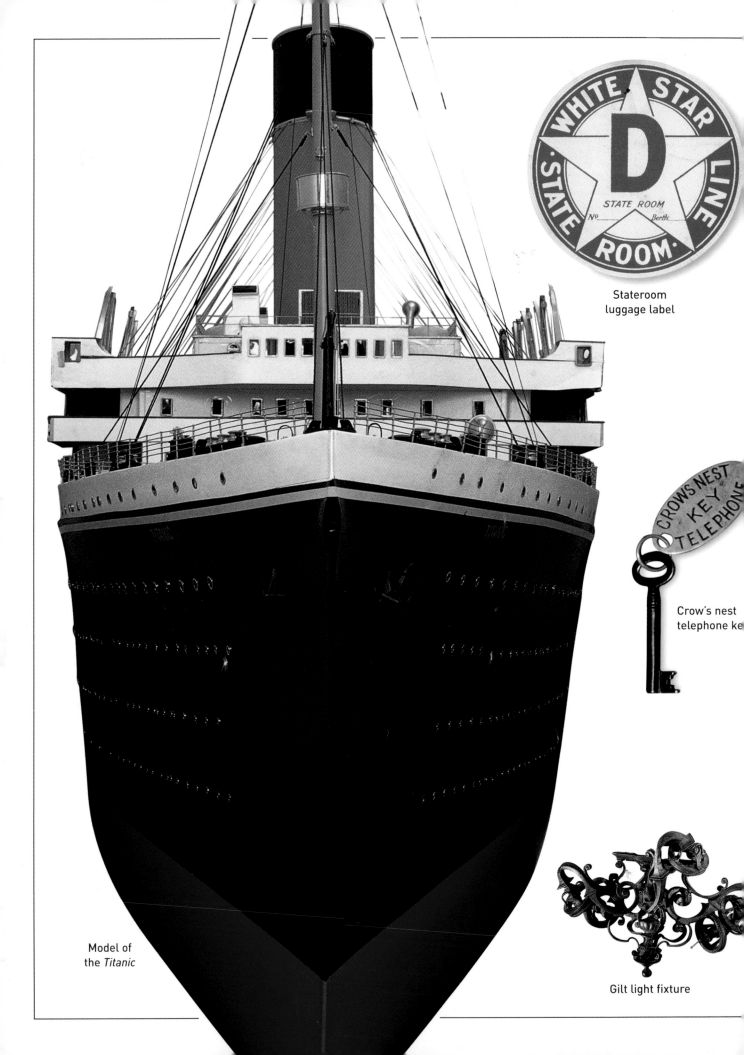

STATE ROOM

WHITE STAR LINE

D

STATE ROOM

Nᵒ̲̲̲̲̲̲̲̲ Berth

Stateroom
luggage label

Crow's nest
telephone ke

Model of
the *Titanic*

Gilt light fixture

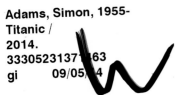

First-class faucets

Bell from crow's nest

EYEWITNESS
TITANIC

Written by
SIMON ADAMS

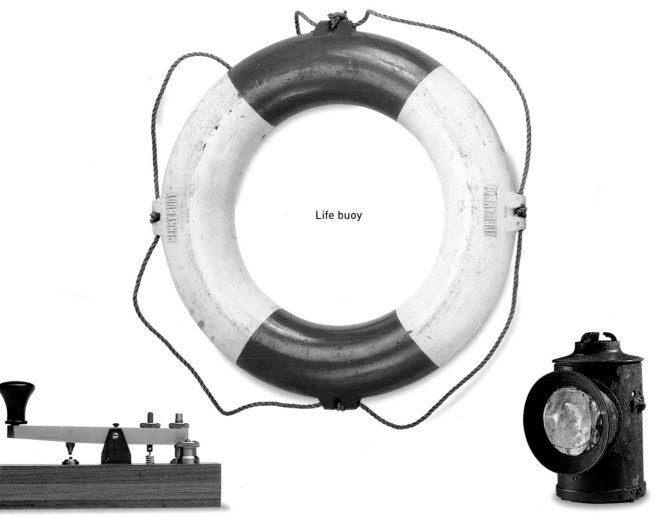
Life buoy

Morse-code transmitter

Passageway lamp

Compass head

Porthole

Captain Smith

DK

LONDON, NEW YORK,
MELBOURNE, MUNICH, AND DELHI

Project editor Melanie Halton
Art editor Mark Regardsoe
Designer Polly Appleton
Senior managing editor Linda Martin
Senior managing art editor Julia Harris
Production Kate Oliver
Picture researcher Claire Taylor
DTP Designer Andrew O'Brien

RELAUNCH EDITION (DK UK)
Editor Ashwin Khurana
US editor Margaret Parrish
Senior designers Rachael Grady, Spencer Holbrook
Managing editor Gareth Jones
Managing art editor Philip Letsu
Publisher Andrew Macintyre
Producer, preproduction Adam Stoneham
Senior producer Charlotte Cade
Jacket editor Maud Whatley
Jacket designer Laura Brim
Jacket design development manager Sophia MTT
Publishing director Jonathan Metcalf
Associate publishing director Liz Wheeler
Art director Phil Ormerod

RELAUNCH EDITION (DK INDIA)
Senior editor Neha Gupta
Art editors Deep Shikha Walia, Shreya Sadhan
Senior DTP designer Harish Aggarwal
DTP designers Anita Yadav, Pawan Kumar
Managing editor Alka Thakur Hazarika
Managing art editor Romi Chakraborty
CTS manager Balwant Singh
Jacket editorial manager Saloni Talwar
Jacker designers Govind Mittal, Suhita Dharamjit,
Vikas Chauhan

First American Edition, 1999
This American Edition, 2014
Published in the United States by DK Publishing
4th floor, 345 Hudson Street
New York, New York 10014

14 15 16 17 18 10 9 8 7 6 5 4 3 2 1
196449—07/14

A catalog record for this book is available from the Library of Congress.
ISBN 978-1-4654-2057-2 (Paperback)
ISBN 978-1-4654-2099-2 (ALB)

DK books are available at special discounts when purchased in bulk for sales
promotions, premiums, fund-raising, or educational use. For details, contact:
DK Publishing Special Markets, 345 Hudson Street, New York, New York 10014 or
SpecialSale@dk.com.

Color reproduction by Alta Image Ltd., London, UK
Printed and bound by South China Printing Co. Ltd., China

Discover more at
www.dk.com

Logometer

Memorial badge

Compass stand

Contents

White Star Line
playing cards

Ocean travel

In the days of sail, ships took weeks, if not months, to travel between continents. The development of large, fast steamships during the mid-1800s allowed people to cross the ocean more quickly and cheaply than ever before. Shipyards started to build vast, luxurious passenger ships called liners to attract high-paying passengers. It was into this competitive world that the *Titanic* was launched.

Statue of Liberty overlooks New York Harbor

Red Star Line

The Red Star Line ran steamships fr[om] Belgium to America. The line was par[t of] the International Mercantile Marin[e] Company, which also owned the Wh[ite] Star Line, soon to build the *Titanic*.

Liberty beckons

Many of the steerage (third-class) passengers on board the North Atlantic liners were escaping poverty and oppression in Europe. Between 1900 and 1914, more than 12 million people sailed from Europe to start a new life in the Americas.

Sirius

The first ship to cross the Atlantic entirely under steam power was the paddle steamer *Sirius*. It left London for New York in March 1838, stopping to collect 40 passengers in Queenstown, Ireland. During the 18-day crossing, the crew had to burn furniture and the emergency mast when the ship ran short of coal.

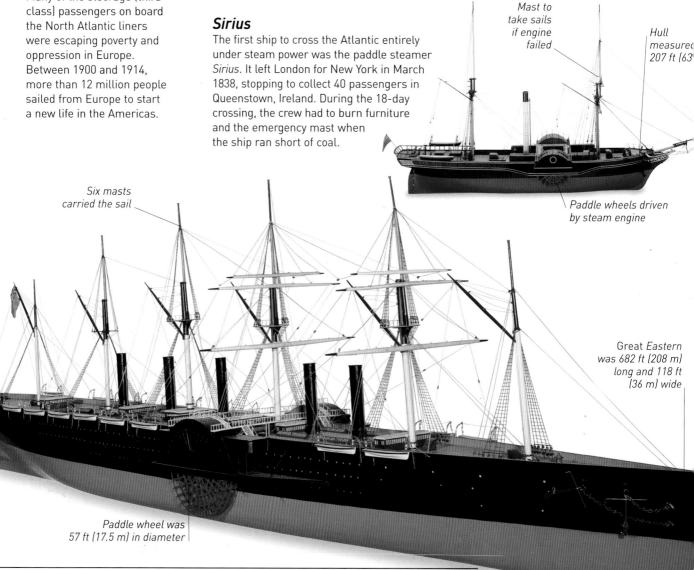

Mast to take sails if engine failed

Hull measured 207 ft (63 [m])

Paddle wheels driven by steam engine

Six masts carried the sail

Great Eastern was 682 ft (208 m) long and 118 ft (36 m) wide

Paddle wheel was 57 ft (17.5 m) in diameter

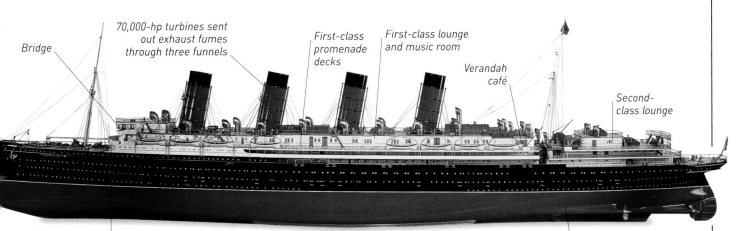

Bridge

70,000-hp turbines sent out exhaust fumes through three funnels

First-class promenade decks

First-class lounge and music room

Verandah café

Second-class lounge

Observation room

Mauretania

With its four giant steam turbines, the *Mauretania* was the pride of the Cunard Line (below left). In 1907, the *Mauretania* set a new record for crossing the Atlantic—four days and 19 hours, at an average speed of 27.4 knots (31.5 mph/50.7 kph). The record went unchallenged until 1929.

The Mauretania *was 748 ft (228 m) long and weighed 35,000 tons (32,000 metric tons)*

White Star Line

Founded in 1871 by shipowner Thomas Ismay, the White Star Line grew from a bankrupt fleet of clipper ships operating between Britain and Australia.

Ornate marble pillars

he Cunard Line

1839, Samuel Cunard established shipping line to take mail from England Canada. The Cunard Line soon came a rival for the White Star Line.

"Everything has been done in regard to the urniture and fittings to make the first-class accommodation more than equal to that provided in the finest hotels on shore."

EXTRACT FROM *THE SHIPBUILDER*

Luxury liners

No expense was spared in decorating the Atlantic liners. For first-class passengers, the public rooms and cabins were often furnished in the style of great country houses, with hardwoods, marble, and gilt. For second-class passengers, the rooms were more than adequately furnished, while many third-class passengers were introduced to good standards of hygiene and table linen for the first time in their lives.

Shipping tycoon

US industrialist John Pierpont Morgan was one of the richest men of his time. In 1902, he bought a number of European shipping lines and created the International Mercantile Marine Company that came to dominate shipping across the North Atlantic.

Building the *Titanic*

Ever since its foundation in 1871, the White Star Line had ordered its new ships from the Harland and Wolff shipyard in Belfast, Northern Ireland. The construction skills of the yard were outstanding, and the workforce took great pride in their ships. Construction of the *Titanic* began on March 31, 1909. First, the keel plates were positioned. Then, when the framework was in place, the beams, deck plates, and hull plates were installed. By May 1911, less than two years after work began, the *Titanic* was ready to be launched.

Thriving workforce
Harland and Wolff doubled its usual workforce about 6,000 people to cope with the construction and fitting out of the *Titanic* and its sister ship, the *Olympic*. Most of the workers lived in the maze of streets surrounding the dockyard.

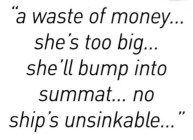

Entrepreneur
Lord William Pirrie, chairman of Harland and Wolff, had worked for the company since 1862. In 1907, Lord Pirrie and Bruce Ismay, chairman of the White Star Line, devised a plan to build three magnificent liners. With the emphasis on luxury and safety, the liners would transform transatlantic travel.

*"a waste of money...
she's too big...
she'll bump into
summat... no
ship's unsinkable..."*

SIR J. BISSET

Under construction
The *Olympic* (right) and the *Titanic* (left) were so big that special slipways had to be built. A central crane and 16 movable cranes were also installed.

Anchor weighed 17 tons (15.75 metric tons)

In dry dock

After its launch on May 31, 1911, the *Titanic* went to the fitting-out basin, where the ship's machinery was installed and the inside of the ship was completed. On February 3, 1912, the *Titanic* went to the dry dock (below), where the propellers were added and a final coat of paint was applied.

...ant anchor

...e *Titanic*'s central anchor was the biggest of the ...p's three anchors. It took a team of 20 horses to ...ul it to the shipyard. The two side anchors were ...f the weight of the central anchor and were ...vered by 107 tons (97.5 metric tons) of cable.

The central propeller shaft awaits the huge, bronze propeller

Driving force

Three huge turbine shafts connected the engines to the propellers at the rear of the ship. The outer propellers had three blades, while the central propeller had four.

Cast in bronze

The two outer propellers measured 23 ft 5 in (7 m) in diameter, while the central propeller was 16 ft 5 in (5 m). Because it was made of bronze, the starboard propeller (above) remained well preserved after the ship sank.

"Unsinkable"?

Despite popular belief, the *Titanic*'s designers never claimed the ship was unsinkable or exceptionally fast. Its owners claimed that the ship's system of watertight bulkheads (wall-like partitions) "made the vessel virtually unsinkable." The word "virtually" was soon forgotten, however, as the sheer size and luxury of the *Titanic* led most people to believe that the ship truly was unsinkable.

Massive A-frame supports engine

Shipyard worker dwarfed by colossal engine

Mighty engines

The *Titanic* was driven by two massive steam engines that stood more than 30 ft (9 m) tall. Steam from these two monsters passed into a 470-ton (427-metric-ton) turbine engine, then traveled along the turbine shaft, providing the power to drive the central propeller.

Letting off steam

Each engine had four huge cylinders through which steam passed to drive the propellers. Some of the cylinders survived on the seabed after the ship sank.

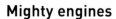

Some boilers weighed more than 110 tons (100 metric tons)

Giant boilers

The ship's engines were powered by 29 boilers, containing 159 furnaces. The furnaces used 728 tons (660 metric tons) of coal a day, driving the ship at a top speed of about 23 knots (26 mph/ 42 kph). Here, the boilers are seen lined up in the boiler shop before being installed in the ship's hull.

Watertight doors

The *Titanic*'s bulkheads contained a series of watertight doors. Only 12 of these doors, at the bottom of the ship, could be closed electrically from the bridge. The other 30 had to be closed by hand. After the collision, a few of these manually operated doors were closed, some were left open, and others were reopened to set up water pumps.

Watertight doors drop into place to seal bulkheads

33-ft (10-m) gaping hole in Arizona's crumpled bow

Surviving the ice

In 1879, *Arizona*—the largest liner of its day—hit an iceberg head-on off the coast of Newfoundland. The bow shattered, but the ship managed to limp backward to Newfoundland without casualties.

The Titanic*'s 15 bulkheads separated its hull into compartments*

"I cannot imagine any condition which would cause a ship to founder. I cannot conceive of any vital disaster happening to this vessel."

CAPTAIN SMITH

The bulkheads

The *Titanic*'s 15 watertight bulkheads divided the ship into 16 compartments. In theory, the ship would still float with two compartments flooded, or even with all four of the smaller bow compartments flooded. However, the bulkheads reached only 10 ft (3 m) above the waterline, which meant that water could still slop over from one compartment to another if the ship was sinking.

Launch
OF
White Star Royal Mail Triple-Screw Steamer
"TITANIC"
At BELFAST,
Wednesday, 31st May, 1911, at 12.15 p.m.
Admit Bearer.

Privileged viewers

Most people viewed the launch of the *Titanic* from the banks of the Lagan River, Belfast, but those who had tickets could watch the events from within the dock.

Launch time

The *Titanic* was launched, with little fanfare, at 12:14 p.m. on May 31, 1911. Lubricated with soft soap, tallow (animal fat), and tallow mixed with oil, the ship took 62 seconds to slide into the water. Once afloat, tugs pulled it toward its fitting-out berth, just as they had done with the *Olympic* (left) seven months earlier.

RMS *Titanic*

Almost identical to its sister ship, the RMS *Olympic*, the *Titanic* was truly vast. The ship could carry up to 3,547 passengers and crew. When fully laden, the *Titanic* topped 73,924 tons (67,063 metric tons) making it the heaviest ship afloat at that time. The style and luxury of the internal fittings meant that it was also the finest. Its title of RMS—Royal Mail Ship—was highly suitable for such a regal ship.

Titanic postcard, 1912

Big ship

The sheer size of the *Titanic* remains impressive to this day, but so too does the design. The hull was sleek and sheer, dominated by four huge funnels. The two wooden masts were used only as flagpoles for the ensigns (flags) and as supports for the wireless antenna.

Ensign of the White Star Line

Wireless antenna strung between two masts

Backstay to hold up rear mast

Rear mast

Aft deck for use by third-class passengers

Second-class enclosed promenade

Docking bridge for use by crew when ship docking in port

Poop deck for use by third-class passengers

Blue Ensign of the Royal Naval Reserve

Third-class cabins in noisy rear of ship

Cast-steel rudder

Central, ahead-only, four-bladed propeller made of bronze

Three-bladed side propeller of bronze

Double-bottomed hull

How long?

The distance from the ensign mast at the stern to forestay fitting at the bow was 882 ft 9 in (269.1 m), or the length of 22 buses.

Breath of fresh air

Passengers could stretch their legs and enjoy the sea air on the boat decks. Deckchairs were available for those wishing to sit and relax, although the lifeboats restricted the view of the sea.

"Perhaps the most striking features... are the four giant funnels—huge tawny brown and black capped elliptical cylinders of steel which tower 175 ft (53 m) from the keel plate, dominating the other shipping in the port, and dwarfing into insignificance the sheds on the quayside."

EXTRACT FROM THE *SOUTHAMPTON PICTORIAL*

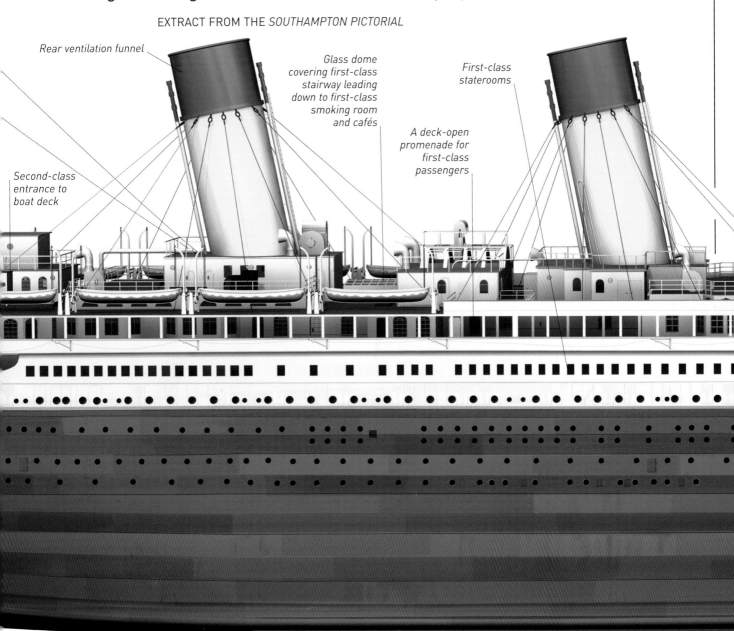

Rear ventilation funnel

Glass dome covering first-class stairway leading down to first-class smoking room and cafés

First-class staterooms

A deck-open promenade for first-class passengers

Second-class entrance to boat deck

On the bridge

Situated at the front of the boat deck, the bridge was the command center of the ship. From this viewpoint, the captain and his officers surveyed the sea in front and sent orders to the engine room. Although the ship was steered from the wheelhouse, the captain also had a small wheel on the bridge that he could use in case of emergencies.

Portholes

Portholes lined the sides of the ship from the first-class suites on C deck down to the third-class berths on the lower deck. The portholes allowed light and fresh air into the cabins and lit up the hull at night.

"Like the Olympic, yes, but so much more elaborate. Take the dining salon—Olympic didn't even have a carpet but the Titanic—ah, you sank in it up to your knees."

BAKER REGINALD BURGESS

Forward grand staircase leading down to first-class dining salon

Gymnasium for first-class passengers

Compass platform for navigation

A deck-enclosed promenade for first-class passengers

Officers' quarters on the boat deck

Lifeboat hanging on its davits (steel arms)

One of four collapsible lifeboat

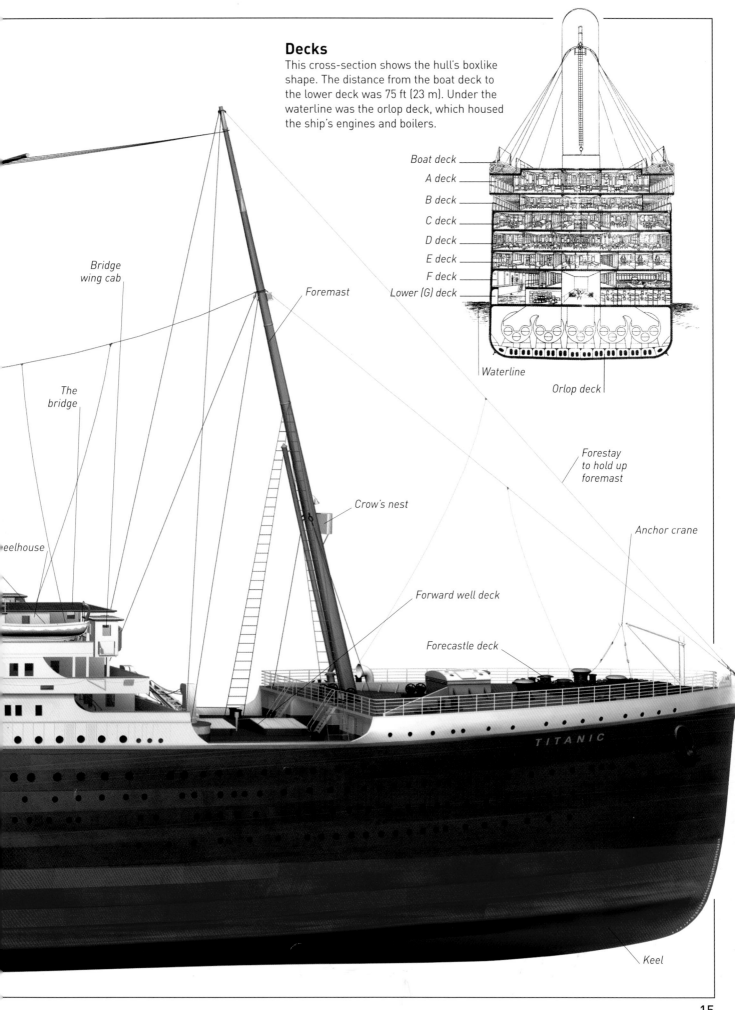

Decks

This cross-section shows the hull's boxlike shape. The distance from the boat deck to the lower deck was 75 ft (23 m). Under the waterline was the orlop deck, which housed the ship's engines and boilers.

Boat deck

A deck

B deck

C deck

D deck

E deck

F deck

Lower (G) deck

Waterline

Orlop deck

Bridge wing cab

Foremast

The bridge

Forestay to hold up foremast

eelhouse

Crow's nest

Anchor crane

Forward well deck

Forecastle deck

TITANIC

Keel

Fine fixtures

In its fitting-out basin, the *Titanic* was transformed into a floating palace in little more than eight months. No expense was spared in making the *Titanic* the most luxurious liner afloat. All the fixtures were bought brand-new or specially made for the ship; and everything was designed to keep the passengers comfortable and entertained during the trip.

Proud to supply
The *Titanic*'s suppliers were proud to associate themselves with the ship. The message in this ad was clear: you too can share some of the *Titanic*'s luxury, even if you cannot afford to sail on it.

Washed up
Some of the thousands of white dishes on board ship survived the crash, remaining in neat rows just as they were originally stacked.

Gold-plated and crystal light fixtures lit up each landing of the grand staircase

Painter adds highlights to features on a decorative column

Rails of wrought iron and gilt bronze

Finishing touches
This photograph shows expert plasterers and decorators at work on the *Titanic*'s sister ship, the *Olympic*. Period detail was lovingly re-created in the first-class rooms and cabins.

Ornate columns of polished oak

Late 17th-century-style cherub lamp support

Grand staircase
The grand staircase led from the first-class dining salon on D deck up to the first-class promenade deck. The staircase was lit from above by natural light through a glass dome and illuminated at night by gold-plated crystal lights.

tap

ry cabin had running
ter, a luxury few of the
rd-class passengers
uld have enjoyed at
ne. There were,
vever, only two
htubs for the 710
rd-class passengers.

*First-class
tub faucets
recovered from
the Titanic
wreck site*

On the verandah
One of the most popular rooms on board was
the verandah café. The café was light and
airy with wicker furniture, a checkered floor,
and ivy growing up trellises on the walls.

Reading room
With plenty of space and
comfortable chairs, the
white-paneled reading
room was an ideal place
to write a letter or read
a book, a selection of
which was available from
the ship's large library.

*Clock surrounded
by two figures
symbolizing
Honor and Glory
crowning Time*

*Gilt light fixture
crumpled in wreck*

Light fantastic
The gilt light fixtures in the
first-class lounge matched the
Louis XVI style of the room.

Uplifting
Three elevators took first-class passengers from the
promenade deck down five decks to their cabins. The
elevators were magnificently decorated and disguised
behind pillars. An elevator near the stern of the ship
was available to second-class passengers.

Captain and crew

Hidden from view was a vast army of workers who kept the ship running. Engineers, chefs, barbers, and many others slaved away on the lower decks. On the public decks, steward, pursers, and waiters looked after the passengers. In total, there were 898 crew members, including the captain and his senior officers, who were responsible for every aspect of life on board.

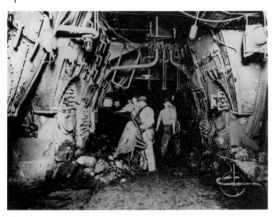

The stokers
Working in shifts, the 289 firemen and stokers shoveled coal into the boilers to keep the engines working at full speed. Many of the workers sang as they worked to keep their spirits up.

The power houses
A team of 28 engineers ran the ship's boiler rooms that were hot, noisy, and dirty. If the boilers ran out of coal or stopped working, the ship would grind to a halt.

Chief Purser Herbert McElroy

Second Officer Charles Lightoller

Third Officer Herbert Pitman

Fourth Officer Joseph Boxhall

Fifth Off. Harold L

Sixth Officer James Moody

Chief Officer Henry Wilde

Captain Edward Smith

First Officer William Murc

The officers
This photograph shows the captain and his officers on board the *Titanic*. The stripes on the sleeves show an individual's rank—the more stripes, the more senior the officer.

Sam Collins
While on board the *Carpathia*, fireman Sam Collins (above) befriended the young Frankie Goldsmith, whose father went down with the *Titanic*. Frankie had enjoyed watching the firemen in the *Titanic*'s engine rooms.

Loading mail sacks onto the *Titanic*

Mail ship
The *Titanic* was carrying mail for the British Royal Mail. Mail sacks were stored in the hold with the luggage. The five clerks working in the hold were among the first to notice water pouring in through the hull.

Pocket watch stopped at 2:16 a.m.; the ship finally sank at 2:20 a.m.

[ru]sty [pe]nknives

Mechanical pencil

Recovered life

First-class steward Edmund J. Stone was responsible for staterooms E1 to E42. His body was one of the first to be recovered by the *Mackay-Bennett*, and he was buried at sea. Stone's personal belongings (left) were returned to his widow after his death.

At your service

The first-class restaurant was run by Monsieur Gatti, the owner of an exclusive French restaurant in London. Only one of his team of 55 cooks and waiters survived the tragedy.

"The night before sailing I asked my wife to put my white star in my cap, and while she was doing it the star fell all to pieces. With a look of dismay she said, 'I don't like this.'"

STEWARD ARTHUR LEWIS

Violet Jessop

Annie Robinson

Some of the surviving stewardesses pictured on their arrival in Plymouth, England

[Th]e stewardesses

[Ou]t of a crew of 898, there were only 18 stewardesses. Attitudes [to]ward women at that time meant that shipping companies employed [mo]stly male staff. But the "women and children first into the lifeboats" [rul]e ensured that 17 of the stewardesses survived the disaster.

Children's toys hang from the ceiling

Reclining chair

Souvenir pennants

Barber shops

Two barber shops (one in first class, the other in second) offered men a daily hot lather and shave. The shops also sold toys, postcards, and other souvenirs.

On record

Fireman William Nutbeam was one of only 35 out of the 167 firemen to survive the voyage. His logbook states "vessel lost" against the *Titanic* entry.

Predicting the tragedy

There are many strange stories relating to the *Titanic*. Some are tales of prediction that uncannily described the real-life events of the tragedy. A number of people had recurring dreams of the forthcoming collision, and a dying girl in Scotland related the events of the disaster just hours before they unfolded. Several people had such strong premonitions that they refused to board the *Titanic*. Others were simply very lucky and failed to board on time.

Collision visions
New York lawyer Isaac Frauenthal had a dream about the disaster before boarding the *Titanic*, and again when he was on board the ship. Unlike other passengers, he wasted no time boarding a lifeboat when he heard about the collision.

Collision occurred below the waterline, some 85 ft (26 m) from the stern

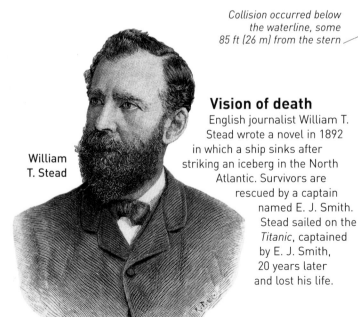

William T. Stead

Vision of death
English journalist William T. Stead wrote a novel in 1892 in which a ship sinks after striking an iceberg in the North Atlantic. Survivors are rescued by a captain named E. J. Smith. Stead sailed on the *Titanic*, captained by E. J. Smith, 20 years later and lost his life.

A bad ome
A warning of the forthcoming tragedy occurred
September 20, 1911, when the *Titanic*'s sister ship, t
Olympic, collided with the warship HMS *Hawke*. Both sh
were badly damaged, and the *Olympic*, under E. J. Smi
soon to captain the *Titanic*, was found to be at fa

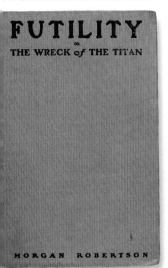

Futility

In 1898, Morgan Robertson wrote a novel called *Futility* in which a ship tries to cross the Atlantic in record time, hits an iceberg, and sinks with the loss of almost all of its passengers due to a shortage of lifeboats.

Jessie's dream

On April 14, 1912, a dying Scottish girl named Jessie had a vision of a ship sinking and "someone called Wally... playing a fiddle." Within hours of her death, the *Titanic* slowly sank as Wally Hartley and the rest of the band continued to play.

Reverend J. Stuart Holden's unused ticket

Ceramic figurine coated with turquoise glaze (around 700 BCE)

Pharaoh's luck

First-class passenger Molly Brown grabbed her lucky Egyptian statuette as she left the cabin. It stayed with her until she was rescued by the *Carpathia*.

Lucky escape

Among the 55 passengers who canceled their bookings at the last moment was John Pierpont Morgan, owner of the White Star Line and the *Titanic* itself. Reverend J. Stuart Holden of London escaped the disaster because his wife became ill.

History repeats

In April 1935, the steamer *Titanian* met an iceberg in the same area as the *Titanic* had done 23 years earlier. Crew member William Reeves had a premonition seconds before the iceberg came into view and yelled "Danger ahead!" to the navigator, who quickly reversed the engines and stopped the ship.

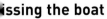

Missing the boat

Many crew members were recruited in the pubs of Southampton, England. However, 22 recruits failed to board the ship, notably the three Slade brothers, who were prevented from reaching the ship by a long freight train passing through the docks.

The Belvedere Arms, a pub in Southampton where people were recruited to work on the Titanic

Maiden voyage

A new ship's first voyage—its maiden journey—is always an important occasion. The *Titanic* arrived in Southampton on April 3, 1912. For the next few days, the docks bustled with activity as the crew arrived and supplies were loaded on board. On the morning of April 10, passengers boarded the ship. At noon, the ship slipped its moorings and the voyage had begun.

South Western Hotel
A number of wealthy passengers spent the night before the voyage in the South Western Hotel, Southampton, overlooking *Titanic*'s dock.

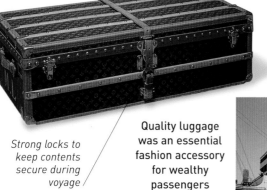

Strong locks to keep contents secure during voyage

Quality luggage was an essential fashion accessory for wealthy passengers

All aboard
On the morning of the *Titanic*'s departure, huge crowds gathered to wave goodbye to friends and relatives.

White Star Line's Southampton pier teems with life on the morning before the Titanic *departs*

Sea trial
Before it left Belfast for Southampton, the *Titanic* went through a series of sea trials. The engines were tested, and different speeds were tried out. The crew also conducted an emergency stop, bringing the ship to a halt in 0.6 miles (1 km) from a speed of 20 knots (23 mph/37 kph).

Rear funnel was for show only, so it never actually belched out smoke

Tugs escort the Titanic *out of its dock to begin sea trials*

Channel hopping

The *Titanic* stopped first at Cherbourg, France, where more passengers got on. It then recrossed the English Channel to Queenstown (now Cobh), Ireland. On April 11, the *Titanic* finally left Europe for New York.

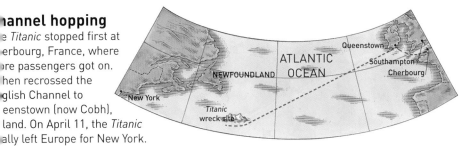

Farewell to Europe
At Queenstown, the *Titanic* picked up seven second-class and 113 steerage (third-class) passengers, many of whom were leaving Ireland to start a new life in the US.

The New York *escapes crashing into the* Titanic

"The ship is so big that I have not yet found my way about. I hope I shan't get lost on board before I arrive in New York!"

A PASSENGER

A near miss

As tugs pulled the *Titanic* out of its dock, wash from the ship's engines caused the *New York* to swing out in front of the *Titanic*. Quick action by the tugs prevented a collision, but it was a bad start to the voyage.

First class

With most of the top four decks reserved for their use only, the 329 first-class passengers sailed in lavish comfort, with a vast workforce ready to cater to their every need. When not resting in their cabins, first-class travelers had the use of a squash court, a gymnasium, a swimming pool, a library, and a range of dining rooms, bars, and restaurants.

The Astors
With a personal wealth of around $87 million in 1912, Colonel John Jacob Astor IV was the wealthiest passenger on board. Recently divorced, the 46-year-old was returning to New York with his 18-year-old second wife, Madeleine.

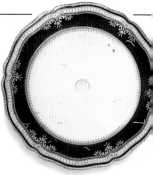

At their service
In addition to elegant plates, the first-class diners had use of 1,500 champagne glasses, 100 pairs of grape scissors, and 1,000 finger bowls.

R.M.S. "TITANIC

APRIL 14, 1912.

LUNCHEON.

Consommé Fermier   Cockie Leekie

Fillets of Brill

Egg à l'Argenteuil

Chicken à la Maryland

Corned Beef, Vegetables, Dumplings

FROM THE GRILL.

Grilled Mutton Chops

Mashed, Fried & Baked Jacket Potatoes

Custard Pudding

Apple Meringue   Pastry

BUFFET.

Salmon Mayonnaise   Potted Shrimps

Norwegian Anchovies   Soused Herrings

Plain & Smoked Sardines

Roast Beef

Round of Spiced Beef

Veal & Ham Pie

Virginia & Cumberland Ham

Bologna Sausage   Brawn

Galantine of Chicken

Corned Ox Tongue

Lettuce   Beetroot   Tomatoes

CHEESE.

Cheshire, Stilton, Gorgonzola, Edam, Camembert, Roquefort, St. Ivel, Cheddar

Iced draught Munich Lager Beer 3d. & 6d. a Tankard.

À la carte
This menu for the last luncheon served on the *Titanic* shows the choice of dishes offered. The first-class dining room could seat more than 550 people.

Starched white linen napkins and tablecloths

Tables decorated with fresh flowers and baskets of fruit

Dinner and dance
The seven-course evening meal was the social highlight of the day. Women wore their finest new gowns from Paris; the men wore tuxedos. After the meal, the more energetic passengers took to the dance floor, although dancing was not allowed on Sundays. Other m retired to the smoking rooms and women to the various lounges.

Luggage labels

Every item of luggage was carefully labeled. First-class passengers often took large quantities of belongings. Mrs. Charlotte Cardoza, for example, traveled with 14 trunks, four suitcases, three crates, and a medicine chest.

Writing desk

In state

The first-class staterooms (private cabins) were very spacious, particularly the two promenade suites on B deck. These suites included a living room, two bedrooms, two dressing rooms, a bathroom, and a private deck.

French Empire-style chairs and table

"My pretty little cabin with its electric heater and pink curtains delighted me... its beautiful lace quilt, and pink cushions, and photographs all round... it all looked so homey."

LADY DUFF GORDON

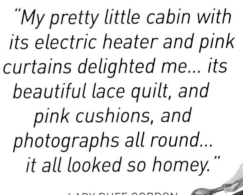

The mechanical camel was especially popular

Keep in shape

The gymnasium contained rowing and cycling machines, weights, and other equipment to keep the first-class passengers fit.

Silver service provided by waiters

Turkish delight

The Turkish baths contained hot, medium, and cool rooms, a shampooing room, and a massage couch, as well as a plunge pool in which to cool off. The baths, like the gymnasium, had separate sessions for men and women.

Second class

On board the *Titanic*, the second-class facilities were far superior to the first-class facilities in most rival liners. The oak-paneled dining salon provided a four-course dinner followed by fruit, cheese, and coffee. Passengers had use of a library, a barber's shop, and a range of bars and salons. The cabins were comfortable, and the open decks provided space for games and relaxation.

Dining in style
This plate from the second-class service shows the strict class structure on board. Each class ate from a different style of plate.

Father and daughter
This photograph shows second-class passengers Robert Phillips and his daughter, Alice, who boarded the *Titanic* at Southampton. Alice survived the disaster, but tragically her father was lost.

Letter home
During the stop in Ireland on April 11, many passengers mailed letters home describing life on board. The writer of this letter reports, "we have been having very rough weather," although the first overnight passage was in fact quite calm.

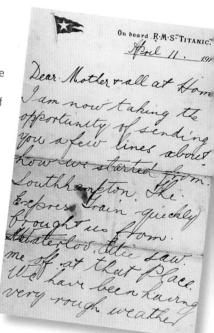

Passengers dwarfed by huge funnels

On deck
The boat deck had plenty of space to relax. A safer ship would have had less room, however, since the deck area would have held extra lifeboats.

Travel blanket to keep out the cold

In the hold

All luggage not needed during the voyage was stored in the hold. Second-class passengers may not have had as much luggage as those in first class, but they would all have traveled with evening wear for dinner.

Second-class label for luggage to be stored in the hold

The Hart family

Benjamin Hart was emigrating to Canada with his wife, Esther, and daughter, Eva. Esther thought the idea of the *Titanic* being "unsinkable" was "flying in the face of God." Convinced of disaster, she slept during the day and kept watch at night. Eva and her mother survived the tragedy, but sadly Benjamin died.

"No effort had been spared to give even second-cabin passengers... the best dinner that money could buy."

A PASSENGER

Basin for washing and shaving

₋unked up

₋quipped with mahogany furniture, the 207 ₋cond-class cabins were more than comfortable. ₋cated on D, E, F, and G decks, the cabins slept ₋o to four passengers in single beds or bunks.

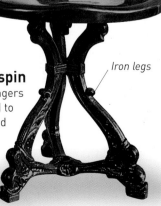

Wooden seat

Iron legs

White Star Line playing cards

Games of risk

Playing cards was a popular pastime on board. But gambling was risky; professional cheats, traveling under ₋ssumed names, hoped to collect big winnings from unsuspecting players.

In a spin

In the dining salon, passengers sat on swivel chairs fixed to the floor. Although the food was prepared in the same kitchen as the first-class meals, the second-class menu was simpler— but no less filling.

Third class

Durable matches
This box of matches bearing the White Star Line logo was recovered from the seabed.

More than half of the total 1,324 passengers—710 in all—were traveling steerage (third class). These passengers came from all over Europe and most were leaving to start a new life in the US. More than 100 of the steerage passengers were Irish. Many had never been to sea before, few had any belongings, and all were leaving home with mixed feelings. On board, 220 cabins housed families, while single people were separated: women in cabins at the rear and men in a large dormitory in the bow.

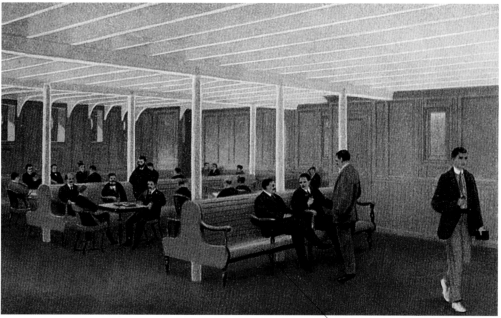

The general room
Paneled with pine and furnished with sturdy benches, tables, and chairs, the general room—the third-class equivalent of a lounge—and the smoking room were the only public rooms available to third-class passengers.

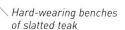
Hard-wearing benches of slatted teak

"We were emigrants, my parents had a public house in London... we were going to Kansas, my father was going to buy a tobacconist's shop."

MILLVINA DEAN

Leather hold-all recovered from the wreck site and restored

Life in a bag
Unlike those in first and second class, most passengers in third class traveled light, having only a few valuables and personal belongings.

Open deck

Buffeted by the wind and blasted by smoke from the ship's funnels, the rear decks allocated to the third-class passengers nevertheless provided a welcome change from the crowded cabins and dining rooms below.

Shift work

Since the dining salon had space for only 473 people, third-class passengers ate in shifts. Dining tickets showed the times of the seatings.

Inspection card

Each emigrant was issued with a green inspection card stating the place of departure and the holder's last country of residence. Thomas Theobald's inspection card (left) shows that he was transferred from the *Adriatic* to the *Titanic*—a move that cost him his life.

The Goodwin family

Frederick and Augusta Goodwin and their six children, including baby Sidney (not shown here), were emigrating from London to the US. None of them survived.

Dining salon

Four-berth cabin

WHITE STAR LINE
ROYAL & STEAMERS
UNITED STATES MAIL

FIRST SAILING OF THE LATEST ADDITION TO THE WHITE STAR FLEET

The Queen of the Ocean

TITANIC

LENGTH 882½ FT. OVER 45,000 TONS BEAM 92½ FT.
TRIPLE-SCREWS

This, the Latest, Largest and Finest Steamer Afloat, will sail from
WHITE STAR LINE, PIER 59 (North River), NEW YORK

Saturday, April 20th At 12 Noon

All passengers berthed in closed rooms containing 2, 4, or 6 berths, a large number equipped with washstands, etc.

THIRD CLASS FOUR BERTH ROOM

THIRD CLASS DINING SALOON

Spacious Dining Saloons
Smoking Room
Ladies' Reading Room
Covered Promenade

Reservations of Berths may be made direct with this Office or through any of our accredited Agents

THIRD CLASS RATES ARE:

To PLYMOUTH, SOUTHAMPTON, LONDON, LIVERPOOL and GLASGOW. | $36.25
To GOTHENBURG, MALMÖ, CHRISTIANIA, COPENHAGEN, ESBJERG, Etc. | 41.50
To STOCKHOLM, ÅBO, HANGÖ, HELSINGFORS | 44.50
To HAMBURG, BREMEN, ANTWERP, AMSTERDAM, ROTTERDAM, HAVRE, CHERBOURG | 45.00
TURIN, $48. NAPLES, $52.50. PIRAEUS, $55. BEYROUTH, $61., Etc., Etc.

DO NOT DELAY: Secure your tickets through the local Agents or direct from
WHITE STAR LINE, 9 Broadway, New York

TICKETS FOR SALE HERE

Two months' pay

This advertisement for the voyage that never happened—the return of the *Titanic* to England—gives a good idea as to the cost of a third-class ticket. At $36.25, the price was equivalent to about two months' wages for most third-class passengers.

Atlantic crossing

As the *Titanic* sped across the North Atlantic on Sunday, April 14, 1912, it received a series of messages from other ships in the area warning of ice. Captain Smith firmly believed that his ship was in no danger, and he was urged on by Bruce Ismay, the ship's owner, to prove the vessel's speed and reliability by arriving ahead of schedule

***Titanic* illuminations**
At night, the *Titanic* shone brightly as the cabin lights glowed and the decks were lit up.

Two clocks show the time at the ship's location and at its destination

Wireless room
The use of wireless radio on board ship was still a novelty at that time. Until the *Titanic* disaster, few people realized the importance of radio a form of emergency communication.

Battery charging pane

Magnetic detector, or "Maggie"

Spark transmitter

Headphones for hearir incoming messages

Morse-code keys for sending messages

Telegraph message pad

Transmitter tuning coil

Fleming valve tuner

Marconi telegraph codes book

Multiple tuner for receiving Morse-code signals

Wireless operator's logbook

Marconi wireless operators
The *Titanic*'s two wireless operators, Jack Phillips and Harold Bride (left), were employed by Marconi rather than the White Star Line. Bride was only 22 years old, and was paid about $25 a month to work the night shift while his senior colleague, Phillips, rested.

To friends and fami
Although most passengers communicated with fam and friends by mail, many wealthy passengers use the *Titanic*'s telegraph. The workload was so heavy th Jack Phillips interrupted the final ice warning from tl *Californian* to continue transmittin

> *"Captain, Titanic—*
> *Westbound steamers*
> *report bergs,*
> *growlers, and field*
> *ice in 42ºN from 49º*
> *to 51ºW, April 12."*

TELEGRAPH FROM CAPTAIN BARR
OF THE *CARONIA*

Warning message

As the *Titanic* steamed ahead, it received nine messages warning of ice. Although not all of the warnings reached the bridge, the message from the German ship *Amerika* (above) was passed to Captain Smith in person.

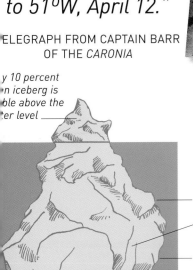

Only 10 percent
of an iceberg is
visible above the
water level

165 ft
(50 m)

Beneath the sea's surface, an iceberg is bulky, with many sharp edges capable of puncturing a ship's hull

330 ft
(100 m)

500 ft
(150 m)

Hidden danger

Often, 90 percent of an iceberg's bulk is hidden beneath the sea. Icebergs are formed when chunks of freshwater ice break away from glaciers and float into the sea. They can be up to 150 miles (240 km) long and 70 miles (110 km) wide, although smaller "growlers" are also common.

Icebergs can tower above the sea like mountains, or lie flat on the water like frozen fields

Bruce Ismay

Bruce Ismay, owner of the *Titanic*, was accompanying the ship on its maiden voyage. He persuaded Captain Smith to speed through the icefield rather than slow down or stop for the night.

Journey of an iceberg

The icebergs of the North Atlantic begin life in the glaciers of the polar icecap and are carried south by the Labrador Sea, between Canada and Greenland. Some are so large that they survive at sea for several years before melting in warmer waters.

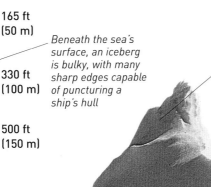

A deadly collision

The night of April 14, 1912, was clear and bitterly cold on the North Atlantic Ocean. The sea was calm and still. Because it was so clear, everyone thought there would be plenty of time to avoid any obstacles. But large ships at full speed do not turn quickly or easily, and when lookout Fredrick Fleet spotted an iceberg, at about 11:40 p.m., it was too late to avoid a collision.

Warning bell is 17 in (43 cm) in diameter

Mast light indicated the ship's direction of travel

Emergency bell
As the iceberg loomed, Fleet struck the crow's nest bell three times— the signal for danger ahead. He also telephoned the bridge.

Fred Fleet
Frederick Fleet, one of six lookouts on board, was on watch in the crow's nest, high up on the foremast. He spotted what he thought was a small iceberg at about 11:40 p.m. and quickly rang the bell.

Missing keys
David Blair, one of the crew who sailed the *Titanic* down from Belfast, was not hired for the ship's maiden voyage. In his rush to pack, he left the ship with the keys to the crow's nest telephone still in his pocket.

Hatch through which lookouts entered and left the crow's nest

On board, few of the passengers felt anything more than a shudder

Fallen foremast
Two lookouts kept constant watch from the crow's nest. Although damaged, it is clearly visible on the foremast.

It was as though we went over bout a thousand marbles."

MRS. STUART J. WHITE, PASSENGER

On the bridge

Although the bridge is the command center of a ship, only four officers were on the *Titanic*'s bridge at the moment of impact. One officer had gone into the officers' quarters, and Captain Smith was in his cabin. Three of these six officers lost their lives in the tragedy.

Out of sight

The *Titanic* struck the iceberg on the starboard (right) side of its hull. The crew could see only slight damage to the upper decks. Below the waterline, however, the iceberg had punched a series of holes along 250 ft (76 m) of the hull.

First Officer Murdoch

William Murdoch was in charge of the bridge at the time of the impact. He ordered the change of direction and closed the watertight doors. Later, he called all the passengers up on deck to evacuate the ship.

At the wheel

Quartermaster Robert Hichens turned the wheel hard to starboard (right), swinging the bow to the port (left) of the iceberg. That was all he had time to do.

Wheel was linked to the steering mechanism in the stern above the rudder

33

To the lifeboats

At 12:05 a.m., 25 minutes after the collision, Captain Smith ordered the lifeboats to be uncovered. For the next two hours, total confusion reigned; there had been no lifeboat drill since leaving Southampton, and no one knew what to do. Not one officer realized that the lifeboats could be lowered fully laden. Had they done so, a total of 1,178 people could have been saved, rather than 706.

Women and children first?
The rule on board all ships at that time was to save women and children first. But some men did escape; in many lifeboats, "first come, first saved" was the rule

"As I was put into the boat, he (Mr. Daniel Marvin) cried to me, 'It's all right, little girl. You go. I will stay.' As our boat shoved off he threw me a kiss and that was the last I saw of him."

TITANIC HONEYMOONER MRS. DANIEL MARVIN

Thomas Andrews
Thomas Andrews, managing director of Harland and Wolff and builder of the *Titanic*, calculated that the ship had two hours, at most, before it sank. However, he failed to point out that the lifeboats could be lowered fully laden.

Buoyancy aid
Life jackets were available for every passenger and crew member. The life jackets were buoyant enough to keep a person afloat, but they were very bulky to wear and offered little protection against the extreme cold.

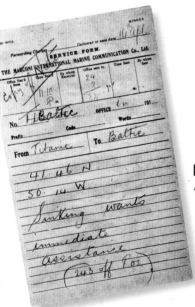

Cork floats covered with thick canvas

In distress
As the lifeboats filled up, the two radio operators tirelessly sent out distress messages asking for help. Among the ships that picked up the *Titanic*'s pleas were the *Olympic*, the *Baltic*, and the *Carpathia*.

...ne by one

...e by one the lifeboats were lowered, starting with
...mber 7 (see below) at 12:45 a.m. and finishing with
...llapsible D at 2:05 a.m. The last two collapsibles
...ated away from the ship as it sank. The total capacity
...all 20 boats was 1,178; it was claimed that about 862
...ople got into a lifeboat. According to the US Senate
...port, however, the number saved was only 706, which
...ggests that some people exaggerated the numbers
...each boat because they had left others to drown.

The collapsibles

Two collapsible lifeboats were stored on
deck, and the other two were stowed
on the roof of the officers'
quarters. The
collapsibles had
flat, double-
bottomed floors
and canvas-
topped sides
that could be
pulled up.

Lifeboat 12 (1:25 a.m.)
Capacity: 65
40 women and children, 2 crew

Lifeboat 10 (1:20 a.m.)
Capacity: 65
48 women and children,
2 men, 5 crew

Lifeboat 4
(1:55 a.m.)
Capacity: 65
35 women and
children, 1 man,
4 crew

Lifeboat 2 (1:45 a.m.)
Capacity: 40
21 women, 1 man, 4 crew

Lifeboat 14 (1:30 a.m.)
Capacity: 65
...women, 2 men, 8 crew

Lifeboat 6 (12:55 a.m.)
Capacity: 65
26 women, 2 crew

Collapsible D (2:05 a.m.)
Capacity: 47
40 women and children,
3 men, 3 crew

Lifeboat 16 (1:40 a.m.)
Capacity: 65
...women, 1 man, 6 crew

Lifeboat 8 (1:10 a.m.)
Capacity: 65
28 women, 4 crew

Collapsible B (2:20 a.m.)
Capacity: 47
Floated upside down with
about 30 men clinging to it

...feboat 15 (1:35 a.m.)
Capacity: 65
...passengers, 13 crew

Lifeboat 7 (12:45 a.m.)
Capacity: 65
8 women, 10 men, 3 crew

Collapsible A (2:20 a.m.)
Capacity: 47
Floated off as the ship sank
1 woman, 10 men, 5 crew

...eboat 13 (1:35 a.m.)
Capacity: 65
55 women and
...dren, 4 men, 5 crew

Lifeboat 11 (1:25 a.m.)
Capacity: 65
60 women and children,
1 man, 9 crew

Lifeboat 5 (12:55 a.m.)
Capacity: 65
41 passengers, 1 crew

Collapsible C (1:40 a.m.)
Capacity: 47
31 women and children,
6 men, 6 crew

Lifeboat 9 (1:20 a.m.)
Capacity: 65
42 women, 6 men,
8 crew

Lifeboat 3 (1:05 a.m.)
Capacity: 65
25 women and children,
10 men, 15 crew

Lifeboat 1 (1:10 a.m.)
Capacity: 40
2 women, 3 men, 7 crew

*Sir Cosmo and
Lady Duff Gordon*

Self-help

Some of the people who failed to board a
lifeboat tried to build their own rafts out
of deckchairs or other buoyant
items. Those flung into the sea
tried desperately to scramble
onto floating wreckage.

...ear collision

...eboats 13 and 15 were lowered
...he same time. Number 13
...ched the water first, but drifted
...o the path of number 15. The
...w had to quickly suspend boat
...in midair until 13 floated away.

Empty vessel

Lifeboat number 1 had only 12 occupants,
including Sir Cosmo and Lady Duff Gordon.
Some people believed they had used their
wealth to secure their own lifeboat and crew.

Slowly sinking

As the lifeboats were lowered, a flurry of activity took place on deck. The radio operators sent out distress signals. Officers on the bridge flashed messages by Morse signal lamp and fired rockets to attract the attention of passing ships. It was hard for many people to believe that the *Titanic* would sink. Some reconciled themselves to their fate, but most believed that help would arrive before the ship went down.

Signaling

Shortly before the first rocket signal was fired, Captain Smith and Fourth Officer Boxhall spotted the lights of a nearby ship. Boxhall tried to attract the ship's attention by flashing the CQD ("come quick, danger") distress signal. But the ship did not respond and it faded from view. New evidence suggests that it may have been a ship illegally hunting seals.

Signaling lamp

Rocket signals explode in the sky

Lighting up the sky

Fourth Officer Boxhall fired the first of about eight rocket distress signals at 12:45 a.m. Each signal—sent up at five-minute intervals—soared 800 ft (244 m) into the air before exploding into a shower of light. Distress signals were always fired at regular intervals so that passing ships would not mistake them for firework displays.

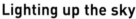

A gentleman

Once the last lifeboat had left, millionaire Benjamin Guggenheim realized that he was not going to be saved. He returned to his cabin, where he and his valet (personal attendant) changed into tuxedos. Before the ship was lost he was heard to say, "We've dressed in our best and are prepared to go down like gentlemen."

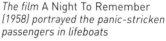

The film A Night To Remember *(1958) portrayed the panic-stricken passengers in lifeboats*

Desperation

As the last lifeboats were lowered, several people tried to get into them by sliding down the ropes or leaping from the lower decks. Others jumped into the sea, hoping to climb aboard later. A few lucky people managed to hide in a lifeboat on deck and were only detected once afloat.

...k Phillips

...first, wireless operator
...k Phillips sent out CQD
...nals. Then at 12:45 a.m.
...sent the new SOS signal—
...first ever to be sent from
...hip in danger.

Final radio message sent by the *Titanic*

CQD = SOS
The first radio distress signal was CQD. In 1906, the SOS signal was created because the letters were easy to transmit by Morse code. Until the *Titanic* disaster, most Marconi operators still used the old signal.

Key is pressed to tap out messages in Morse code

Morse code SOS

Morse code CQD

Communicating in code
Morse code was invented in 1838 by Samuel Morse. Each letter is represented as a series of short or long radio signals or flashes of light.

"It's the new call, and it might be your last chance to send it."

JUNIOR WIRELESS OPERATOR, HAROLD BRIDE, TO JACK PHILLIPS

Lights still illuminate the *Titanic* to draw the attention of any passing ships

Stern rises high out of the water

The final moments

As the *Titanic* slipped lower into the water, those left on board either tried to make rafts from deckchairs and other items of furniture, or prayed for rescue and comforted their loved ones. As the ship plunged deeper into the sea, the stern rose up in the air, causing a wave of passengers to fall off the deck. Out on the ocean, those lucky survivors in the lifeboats looked away as the *Titanic* met its horrific end.

Kate Winslet and Leonardo DiCaprio in the 1997 film *Titanic*

Against the tide
At about 2:15 a.m., water crashed through the glass dome at the top of the grand staircase

Titanic's stern rose up vertically for about 30 seconds before disappearing beneath the sea

Funnels and other equipment on deck broke free and crashed beneath the waves

In time of need
As the ship sank, Father Thomas Byles, a Roman Catholic priest, heard confessions and led prayers at the stern end of the boat deck. Like many of his flock, he lost his life.

Last moments
At 2:18 a.m. the *Titanic's* lights went out. The ship was almost vertical, its bow pointing toward the seabed. The ship snapped between the back two funnels, causing the stern section to break free before it also began to sink. At 2:20 a.m. the *Titanic* finally slipped from view.

Officer Lightoller fires warning shots in the film A Night to Remember *(1958)*

Panic stations

In case of serious disturbances on board, pistols were kept in a safe for use by senior officers. As the lifeboats were launched, gunshots were fired into the air to prevent panicking crowds from swamping the boats.

All alone

The passengers on the lifeboats must have felt very alone in the dark. Many took turns rowing to keep their spirits up and to stay warm.

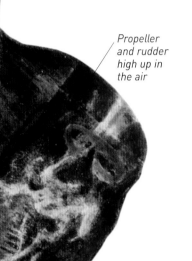

Propeller and rudder high up in the air

"Not until the last five minutes did the awful realization come that the end was at hand. The lights became dim and went out, but we could see. Slowly, ever so slowly, the surface of the water seemed to come up toward us."

ROBERT DANIEL, PASSENGER

Blasted to safety

Colonel Archibald Gracie was dragged underwater by suction from the sinking ship. Then suddenly he was blown clear by a gust of air from a ventilation shaft and managed to climb onto collapsible lifeboat B.

Lifeboats rowed clear of the ship to avoid being dragged down by the ship's suction

Heroic acts

The extreme dangers that the passengers and crew faced led to some remarkable acts of heroism. Down in the boiler rooms, the firemen and stokers worked until the end to keep the lights burning to attract any passing ships. Up on deck, the two wireless operators sent out distress signals for as long as possible. And all the time the band played on.

Countess of Rothes
In lifeboat number 8, the Countess of Rothes took her turn at the oars before handling the tiller for most of the night. She was later presented with the lifeboat number plate mounted on a plaque.

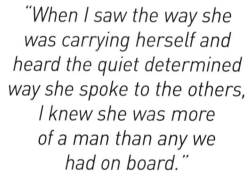

"When I saw the way she was carrying herself and heard the quiet determined way she spoke to the others, I knew she was more of a man than any we had on board."

THOMAS JONES OF LIFEBOAT 8 PRAISES THE COUNTESS OF ROTHES

Molly Brown

US millionairess Molly Brown was one of 26 women on board lifeboat number 6. In charge was Quartermaster Hichens, who refused to let the women row; so Molly Brown took command and rowed furiously toward the rescue ship.

Names of 38 engineers lost with the Titanic

In memoriam
The town most affected by the disaster was Southampton, England, where most of the crew lived. On April 22, 1914, a monument to the ship's engineers was unveiled in the city's East Park. A year later, a smaller memorial to the steward was unveiled on Southampton Common.

And the band played on

The *Titanic* had two bands—a string quintet, led by violinist Wally Hartley, and a string and piano trio that played outside the à la carte restaurant. After the collision, the musicians gathered in the first-class lounge and played a selection of popular songs to keep the passengers' spirits up. They played on until the very end, going down with their ship.

The HEROIC MUSICIANS OF THE TITANIC
who died at their posts like men – April 15th 1912

Extract from the hymn Nearer, My God, To Thee, believed to be the final piece of music played on board

Captain Smith is shown here swimming toward lifeboat B

Captain Smith

The last minutes of Captain Smith's life are largely uncertain because he went down with his ship. Several survivors claimed that he swam close to the upturned collapsible lifeboat B but turned away when he realized how overcrowded its hull was.

Together forever

Wealthy passenger Isidor Straus was the founder of the famous Macy's department store in New York. Because of his age, he was offered the chance to board a lifeboat, but turned it down. His wife, Ida, refused to leave the ship without him.

Engineer at work

Racing to the rescue

At 12:25 a.m. the wireless operator on board RMS *Carpathia* picked up a distress message from the *Titanic*. The ship, en route from New York to the Mediterranean, turned around immediately and sailed 58 miles (93 km) northwest to the distressed liner. Captain Rostron prepared his ship to receive survivors—doctors were put on standby, steward and cooks prepared accommodation and food, and rockets were fired every 15 minutes to signal the ship's approach.

Rowing to safety

The icefield surrounding the survivors meant that it was too dangerous for the *Carpathia* to move in too close. So the exhausted survivors had to row toward the stationary ship. It took four hours to rescue all the survivors.

Ruth Becker

On lifeboat 13, 12-year-old Ruth Becker found herself separated from her mother and younger brother and sister. But she helped to comfort a distraught mother who had been separated from her child. Both were reunited with their families on board the *Carpathia*.

Smoke spewed from Carpathia's funnel as the ship raced to rescue Titanic's survivors

Masthead lights told survivors that help was on its way

In sight

At 4:00 a.m., the *Carpathia* reached the *Titanic*'s last reported position and cut its engines. A green light flickered from lifeboat number 2, where Fourth Officer Boxhall was in charge. Once on board the *Carpathia*, he confirmed the worst to Captain Rostron.

Looking for survivo[rs]

Only one of the lifeboats—number 14, commanded by Fifth Officer Lowe (above)—went back to look for survivors. His boat pulled four people from the sea. All the other boats rowed away because many people feared being sucked down by the sinking ship or swamped by those fighting for their lives in the water.

Survivors burned paper and waved their hands to attract attention

Lifeboats hidden among the floating ice

Electric spark

Out of respect for his abilities, nicknamed the "electric spark," the 42-year-old Captain Arthur Rostron of the *Carpathia* was known for his quick decisions and energetic leadership.

Safe at last

The first survivor, Elizabeth Allen, clambered up a rope ladder to board the *Carpathia* at 4:10 a.m., just under two hours after the *Titanic* sank. Some survivors had to be winched to safety in a wooden seat.

Survivors await their turn to board the Carpathia

Gangway door open to receive survivors

"After we were picked up on the Carpathia my mother came to me, cos every time a lifeboat came I went to see if my father was on it... he wasn't, so my mother turned round and said, 'You've lost your father, you won't see your father any more... he's gone.'"

EDITH HAISMAN

Thank you

Survivors of the disaster joined together to buy a silver cup for Captain Rostron and 320 medals for his crew. The reverse side of each medal bore the crew member's name and an inscription of thanks.

Blankets to keep the survivors warm

Medal shows the Carpathia sailing through ice

All hands on deck

As the survivors clambered on board the *Carpathia*, they were met by passengers and crew offering blankets and hot food and drinks. Some were taken to cabins; others huddled on the deck and tried to come to terms with what had happened.

Awaiting news

A young radio enthusiast in New York picked up the *Titanic*'s distress signals early on Monday, April 15. The signals were also detected in Newfoundland, Canada. The word was out that the *Titanic* was in trouble, but other messages during the day appeared to contradict this. It was not until 6:16 p.m. New York time that it was confirmed that the *Titanic* had sunk.

The worst confirmed
Captain Rostron waited until all the survivors were safely on board before broadcasting any messages. He forwarded a list of survivors, but ignored requests for information from the press until 8:20 p.m.

Waiting for news
As news filtered through, concerned relatives arrived at the White Star offices in New York, Southampton, and London (right). It took some days before the first (incomplete) list of survivors was posted in New York.

For Hascoe, read C. H. Pascoe

For Ross, read H. Ross, cook

Wrong identities
On Wednesday, a list of saved crew members was posted outside the White Star offices in Southampton, where 699 of the 898 crew lived. In the confusion, names were spelled incorrectly and initials omitted, falsely raising some relatives' hopes. Sheets of correct names slowly appeared, confirming who had survived.

Read all about it
People started to realize the scale of the disaster from the cries of the newspaper boys. With no firm news from the White Star Line or the rescue ship, *Carpathia*, worried relatives read the newspapers closely, searching for any scrap of information that might tell them about their loved ones.

"I have read the papers trying to get some hope, but all fail now. I shall pray for the body. He was so good to me."

TITANIC SURVIVOR WRITES ABOUT HER HUSBAND

Monday's New York Evening Sun *reported that all passengers were safe*

Tuesday morning's Chicago Daily Tribune *confirms the full extent of the horror*

Although news of the disaster spread rapidly around the world, it did not always make front page news

round the world

he *Titanic* disaster dominated the newspapers for ays, although many of the early stories were often correct. Most papers erred on the side of caution, t believing that such a disaster could have happened. me even printed that the *Titanic* was being towed Nova Scotia, and that all its passengers were safe.

Good news, bad news

Many women in Southampton lost male relatives in the disaster. Mrs. Rosina Hurst (left) lost her father-in-law, although her husband, fireman Walter Hurst, survived. Sharing the news with her is her aunt, also in mourning clothes.

Lost and found

How many people lost their lives on the *Titanic* will never be known for sure, since the total number of people on board has never been officially established. The US investigation put the total losses at 1,517, while the British inquiry calculated 1,490. But the number of lives tragically lost makes each survivor's story all the more remarkable.

Mrs. Goldsmit wearing tw wedding ring

Memorial badge

Ring twice

As Mrs. Goldsmith stepped into a lifeboat with her son, family friend Thomas Theobald took off his wedding ring and asked her to pass it on to his wife. Sadly Mr. Theobald perishe

Honeymooners Mr. and Mrs. Harder

Horrific honeymoons

Eight newlywed couples chose to take their honeymoon on the *Titanic*'s maiden voyage, although only two of the couples lived to tell the tale.

Survivor Mrs. Clara Hays, who lost her husband, Charles Hays, president of Canada's Grand Trunk Railroad

Baby Millvina

Just seven weeks old at the time of the disaster, Millvina Dean was the youngest survivor of the *Titanic* disaster. Her mother, Ettie, and brother, Bert, also survived; her father died

First class

145 women and children survived; 10 women and 1 child died. Of the men, 54 survived and 119 died. Sixty percent survived.

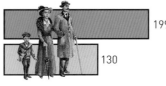 199
130

Under cover

Louis Hoffmann claimed he was taking his orphaned sons to start a new life in America. In fact, his real name was Michel Navratil and he had left his wife and abducted his sons. The boys survived and were later reunited with their mother.

Michel, age 3

Second class

Of women and children, 104 survived, and 24 died. Of the men, 15 survived, and 142 died. Forty-two percent survived.

 119
166

Third class

Of women and children, 105 survived, and 119 died. Of the men, 69 survived, and 417 died. Twenty-five percent survived.

 174
536

Edmond, age 2

Table showing how the death toll varie among the three classes and crew

Saved
Lost

Crew

Of women, 20 survived, and 3 died. Of the men, 194 survived, and 682 died. Twenty-four percent survived.

 214
685

Limping home

On arrival in New York, Harold Bride's feet were so frostbitten that he had to be carried ashore. One of the heroes of the disaster, Bride had continued sending distress signals until minutes before the *Titanic* sank.

Harold Bride's ankles were badly injured during the escape, and his feet were frostbitten

Rest in peace

On April 20, less than a week after the disaster, Canon Kenneth Hind held a funeral service on board the *Mackay-Bennett*. Too disfigured to be identified, 24 people were sewn into weighted sacks and given a dignified burial at sea.

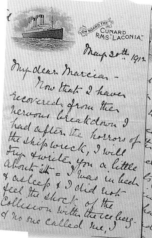

Hat removed out of respect for the dead

Writing home

Many survivors wrote letters to friends or family describing their ordeal. Mary Hewlett, who was in lifeboat number 13, wrote, "I had some long letters I had written to my girls... and I gave them to be burned, sheet by sheet, as signals. The dawn came at about 4:30 a.m.... soon after that we saw the mast lights of the *Carpathia* on the horizon."

At God's service

The Reverend John Harper was on his way from London to hold a series of Baptist meetings in Chicago. Harper's young daughter, Nina, and a relative, Jessie Leitch, both survived, but he went down with the ship.

Body is pulled from the sea into Mackay-Bennett's rowboat

Finding bodies

The gruesome task of collecting bodies was carried out by ships from Halifax, Nova Scotia. The *Mackay-Bennett* carried tons of ice to preserve the bodies and more than 100 coffins. Over the next six weeks, 328 bodies were found.

Lives lost

Every life lost on the *Titanic* was a tragedy. Some of the dead were rich and famous. Many were third-class passengers about to start new lives in the US. Servants traveling with their employers and the many men and women who worked on the ship were all caught up in the terrible event. Few lived to share their stories.

Archibald Butt

Archibald Butt was a US army officer and a military aide to President William Taft. Before the race for the presidential elections in November 1912 began, Butt took a six-week vacation in Europe, returning home on the *Titanic*.

John Thayer

John Borland Thayer was a first-class American cricket player visiting England in 1884 as part of the Philadelphia team. He later became vice president of the Pennsylvania Railroad. In 1912, he and his family went to Europe, coming back on the *Titanic*.

Third-class passengers

One-third of those lost were third-class passengers, many of whom were crossing the Atlantic with hopes for better lives. Some might have achieved great success, but they did not survive to live their dreams.

Passengers boarding the Titanic

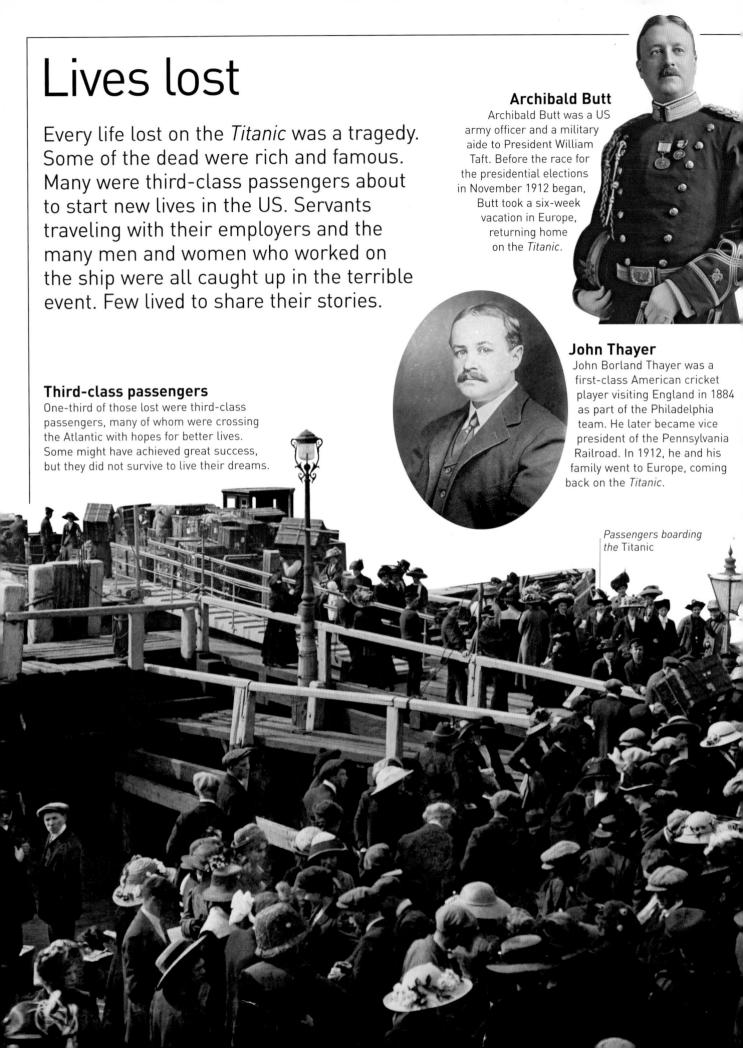

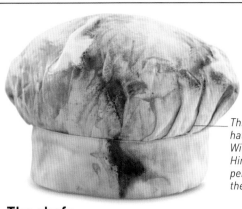
This baker's hat belonged William E. Hine, who perished in the disaster

The chefs

Only 13 of the 62 people who worked in the *Titanic*'s kitchens survived. The à la carte restaurant was run by restaurant owner Luigi Gatti. All 68 staff were employed by Gatti rather than by the White Star Line. Only three survived. It was stated that they were locked into their quarters to stop them from rushing the lifeboats.

Servants

Many first-class passengers brought their valets, maids, chauffeurs, cooks, and nannies with them. Few survived, although some did manage to get aboard a lifeboat, including Mary Anne Perrault, the maid to Mrs. Hays.

Mary Anne Perrault in December 1912

A faraway memorial

In many parts of the world memorials were erected to those who died. In Broken Hill in central Australia, concerned citizens erected a memorial to the heroic bandsmen who played on while the ship sank.

Statue damaged by bombs during World War II

Monument stands 48 ft (14.6) tall

Below decks

All 25 general engineers and the 10 engineers who kept the mechanical equipment running lost their lives. So too did 10 of the 13 leading firemen, of the 73 coal trimmers, 118 of the 163 stokers, and 29 of the 33 greasers. A memorial to the "Engine Room Heroes" was later erected in Liverpool, England (far right).

A still from the German film *Titanic* (1943) showing the ship's engineering crew at work

Survival stories

The lives of many of the survivors were totally changed, and not always for the better. Some thanked their rescuers, others were called cowards, and a few got divorced. Some contributed to the publicity surrounding the event; others refused to talk about their ordeal.

Living on

Most survivors tried to put the tragedy behind them. Those who lived long enough had to relive their memories when the wreck of the *Titanic* was found in 1985.

Madeleine Astor

Madeleine Astor was th pregnant wife of John Jacob Astor IV, who died on the ship. She managed to get into Lifeboat 4 and survived. Later she cohosted a luncheon in New York for Captain Rostron of the *Carpathia* and Dr. Frank McGee, the ship's doctor, to thank them for their help.

The Carters

Lucile Carter, wife of wealthy American William Carter, became a hero for rowing Lifeboat 4. She believed her husband had drowned, only to find him on board the *Carpathia* the next day. In 1914, the couple divorced, with Lucile accusing her husband of having cruelly deserted her and their children on the *Titanic*.

Lifebo

Not all those who survived enjoyed a ha life. Arthur Peuchen, president of Stand Chemical, Iron & Lumber Co. of Canada, offe his services as a yachtsman and was told to on to Lifeboat 6. He found himself with M Brown (see p. 40) and later exaggerated own role. For surviving and boasting abou he was heavily criticized and called a cowa

A lifeboat approaches the Carpathia *that came to help*

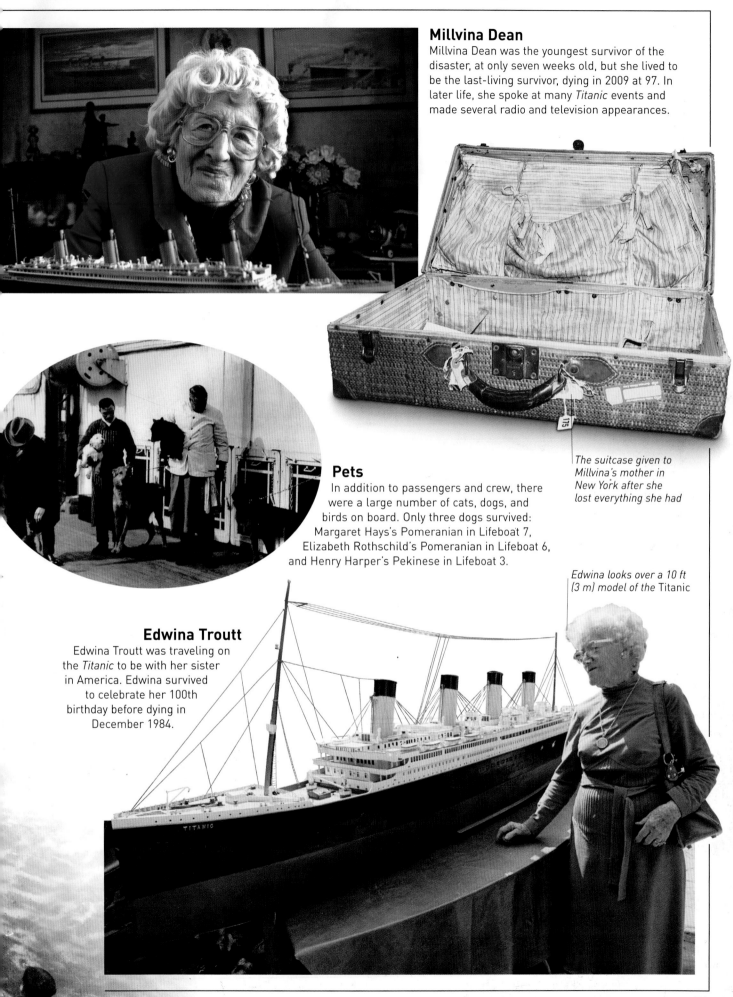

Millvina Dean

Millvina Dean was the youngest survivor of the disaster, at only seven weeks old, but she lived to be the last-living survivor, dying in 2009 at 97. In later life, she spoke at many *Titanic* events and made several radio and television appearances.

The suitcase given to Millvina's mother in New York after she lost everything she had

Pets

In addition to passengers and crew, there were a large number of cats, dogs, and birds on board. Only three dogs survived: Margaret Hays's Pomeranian in Lifeboat 7, Elizabeth Rothschild's Pomeranian in Lifeboat 6, and Henry Harper's Pekinese in Lifeboat 3.

Edwina looks over a 10 ft (3 m) model of the Titanic

Edwina Troutt

Edwina Troutt was traveling on the *Titanic* to be with her sister in America. Edwina survived to celebrate her 100th birthday before dying in December 1984.

Lessons learned

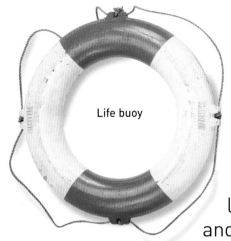

Life buoy

Four days after the *Titanic* sank, the first official inquiry opened in New York, chaired by Senator William Alden Smith. The 82 witnesses included Bruce Ismay, the White Star chairman; Guglielmo Marconi; lookout Frederick Fleet; and Captain Lord of the *Californian*. Two weeks later, the British inquiry began under Lord Mersey. The US inquiry was led by politicians looking for someone to blame, while the British inquiry was led by lawyers and technical experts trying to establish the facts to ensure there was no repetition of the disaster. Both inquiries called for ships to be safer and built to higher standards.

Titanic survivors line up to receive shipwreck pay

Who was to blame?

The US inquiry blamed Captain Smith because of his "overconfidence and neglect." It also blamed Captain Lord of the *Californian*, for not coming to the rescue, and the British Board of Trade for not updating its lifeboat regulations. The British inquiry blamed neither Captain Smith nor the Board of Trade.

The forgotten crew

Under the White Star Line's conditions, the *Titanic*'s crew ceased to be paid at 2:20 a.m. on April 15, the moment the ship sank. Some received expenses, but most were shipped straight home by White Star with little or no financial aid. Many had to rely on emergency shipwreck pay until they could find another job.

The British *Titanic* inquiry in progress

Scale model of the Titanic

Sir Cosmo Duff Gordon gives evidence

Presiding judge, Lord Mersey

Ice patrol

In 1914, to look out for icebergs in the North Atlantic shipping lanes, 16 North Atlantic nations established the International Ice Patrol. Today, the patrol uses ships and airplanes with radar, underwater sonar equipment, and the latest forecasting technology to report the location of icebergs to every ship in the area.

Guglielmo Marconi, inventor of wireless telegraphy

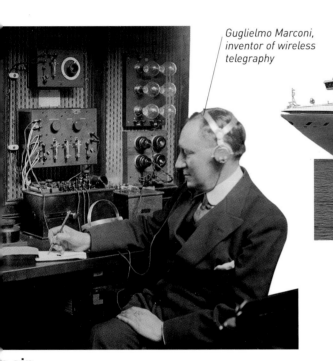

Lifeboats hang beneath the decks of this modern liner, allowing passengers a clear view across the sea

More lifeboats

The main recommendation of both inquiries was that every ship be equipped with enough lifeboats for everyone on board, and that regular lifeboat drills be held. This meant placing more lifeboats on deck, which restricted the passengers' view of the sea.

n air

th inquiries recommended that every ship be uipped with a radio and that radio contact be aintained 24 hours a day. They also advised that all ip radios should follow international regulations.

Last of the line

Although the *Titanic* proved that watertight bulkheads could not stop a ship from sinking, the designers of the Italian liner *Andrea Doria* claimed their ship was unsinkable. But after colliding with the *Stockholm*, in 1956, the ship sank when only one of its 11 compartments flooded. As the bulkhead filled with water, the ship fell to one side, and water poured in above the compartments.

It took several hours for the Andrea Doria *to plunge 240 ft (73 m) beneath the sea*

Not so gigantic
The third of the great White Star Liners was originally called the *Gigantic*, but it was renamed *Britannic* to avoid comparisons with the *Titanic*. With the tragedy in mind, it was outfitted with enough lifeboats for everyone on board.

End of an era

The *Titanic* was meant to be the second in a series of three White Star Line luxury liners. Only one of the three—the *Olympic*—lived up to expectations. The *Titanic* sank, and the *Britannic* was only used for military service. After the *Titanic* tragedy, the *Olympic* was equipped with extra safety measures and cruised the North Atlantic for more than 20 years as both a civilian and a military ship. In 1935, it sailed its final voyage.

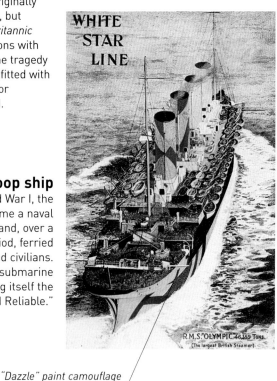

Troop ship
During World War I, the *Olympic* became a naval transport ship and, over a three-year period, ferried 119,000 troops and civilians. It survived three submarine attacks, earning itself the nickname "Old Reliable."

Deck lined with sufficient lifeboats to carry all passengers and crew members

"Dazzle" paint camouflage to confuse enemy submarines

Friends and family wave to passengers aboard the Olympic as it leaves New York

The boom years
The *Olympic* returned to civilian service in July 1920. For the next 15 years, the ship carried many thousands of passengers across the Atlantic. The ship had only one major accident when it struck a lightship in heavy fog in May 1934. Seven of the lightship's 11 crew members were killed. By 1935, the *Olympic* had become dated and later that year it was sold, stripped of its fixtures, and scrapped.

In service

World War I broke out only six months after the *Britannic*'s launch on February 26, 1914. The ship was quickly transformed into a hospital ship, with dormitories and operating rooms on each deck.

Red crosses painted on the side of the hull indicate that the Britannic *is a hospital ship*

Volunteer nurse's uniform

Nurse Jessop

One of the lucky survivors of the *Britannic* disaster was Nurse Violet Jessop (above), who had already escaped death as a stewardess aboard the *Titanic*.

Massive hole ripped out of the Britannic's *port side*

©KEN MARSCHALL 1995

To the seabed

On November 21, 1916, the *Britannic* was sailing northward through the Kea Channel, south of Athens. A sudden explosion ripped the ship open and sank it within an hour. It is thought that the ship struck a mine.

Paneling from the first-class à la carte restaurant of the RMS Olympic

Afterlife

Many of the fixtures from the *Olympic* were removed from the ship before it was scrapped, and they were stored in a barn in England. Rediscovered 56 years later, the fixtures were sold and now furnish hotels, factories, and homes across England.

Search and discovery

Just after midnight on September 1, 1985, scientists on board *Knorr*, the ship searching for the wreck of the *Titanic*, spotted the wreckage of a boiler on the ship's monitors. The camera followed a trail of objects until, suddenly, the huge black shadow of the *Titanic*'s hull came into view. The *Titanic* had been found 73 years after its tragic loss.

The Grand Banks of Newfoundland lie just north of the wreck

Seabed of thick mud strewn with boulders and small rocks

Resting place
The *Titanic* was located at 41°43'N, 49°56'W, 480 miles (770 km) southeast of Newfoundland, Canada, on a sloping seabed overlooking a canyon.

1,650 ft (500 m)

3,300 ft (1,000 m)

Model of the bow section of the *Titanic* wreck

Bow and stern sections cut almost clean apart

6,600 ft (2,000 m)

The wreck
The bow and stern sections of the ship lie 2,000 ft (600 m) apart on the seabed. Both are upright, the bow section having plowed 65 ft (20 m) into the mud.

10,000 ft (3,000 m)

Hostile waters
The *Titanic* lies in 12,500 ft (3,800 m) of water. At this depth, there is no light and the temperature is no more than 36°F (2°C).

Gigantic boilers
As the ship sank, five of its 29 vast boilers broke completely free of the ship and were later found in the field of debris.

Rusty bow
Over the years, layers of rust have covered a fixture on the bow of the *Titanic*, making it appear like a figurehead.

13,000 ft (4,000 m)

Powerful spotlights light the wreck

Nautile

Nautile measured only 27 ft (8 m) in length. Its crew—pilot, copilot, and observer— took 90 minutes to reach the seabed and could stay down for up to eight hours before they had to return to the surface.

cking up the pieces

July 1987, French scientists sailed to the e of the *Titanic* to carry out investigations. e expedition worked from the surface ship *dir* (above), and a crew of three explored the bed in the submersible *Nautile* (right). The w scooped 1,800 objects from the seabed.

Robotic arm for picking up objects

Crew sit inside a titanium sphere

All aboard

Life on board *Nautile* was cramped and hot. Crew members lay on their sides, looking out on the wreck through the small portholes.

Portholes are filled with extra-thick, curved Plexiglas®, which becomes flat due to the water pressure

Foremast lies collapsed over the deck

Anchor crane still stands upright at the bow

Titanic's starboard anchor can still be seen in its original place

ppled telegraph

s telegraph from the docking bridge was d to communicate with the engine room en maneuvering the ship in and out of port.

Peeping into the past

Among the many items picked up from the wreck was one of the ship's portholes. Plates, flatware, and light fixtures were also retrieved from the seafloor.

Nautile's arms have a sucker, a gripper, and a shovel for gathering objects from the seabed

Missing pieces

The discovery of the *Titanic* wreck and the artifacts rescued from the seabed have solved some of the questions that surround the fatal voyage. We now know that the hull broke up as it sank, and that the steel used in its construction was not strong enough to withstand the icy waters of the North Atlantic. We also know that the ship sank some 13 miles (21 km) away from the position estimated at the time of the disaster. This casts doubt on various accounts of which ships were in the area and able to come to the rescue.

Coals from the seabed
Among the items raised from the seabed are pieces of coal that fell from the bunkers. These lumps of coal are the only artifacts from the wreck to have been sold—to raise funds for future salvage efforts.

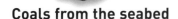
Steel fixture recovered from the wreck site

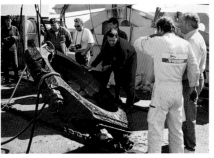

Metal fatigue
Investigation of the steel used in the hull revealed that the plates and rivets became brittle in low water temperatures. On the night of the disaster, the water temperature was about 31°F (–0.2°C). Also, the steel had a high sulfur content, which made it more liable to fracture. This explains why the iceberg caused such serious damage to the hull.

Treasure trove
Many of the artifacts from the wreck were stored in French laboratories and used to help scientists study the harmful effects of seawater. Most of the artifacts have now been carefully restored.

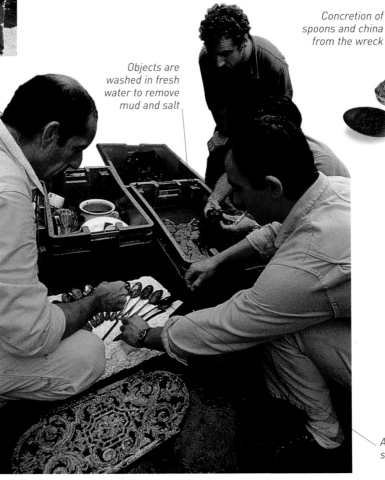

Objects are washed in fresh water to remove mud and salt

Concretion of spoons and china from the wreck

A collection of well preserved spoons recovered from the seab[...]

A new direction
The ship's compass (ab[...] stood on a wooden sta[...] much of which was ea[...] away by marine worm[...] Conservationists hav[...] carefully restored much of the stand.

Fused as one
Seawater produces rust o[...] metal that cements objec[...] into combinations called concretions. Here, spoon[...] and a lump of china have become firmly joined. To separate such objects[...] conservators pass electric[...] through the metal object[...] in a chemical bath, whic[...] softens the concretion.

What happened?

Some eyewitnesses stated that the ship broke in two before it sank; others claimed it went down in one piece. The discovery of the wreck in two pieces, some 2,000 ft (600 m) apart on the seabed, confirms that the hull did indeed break up.

Stage 1
As the "watertight" compartments filled with water, the bow slowly sank, pulling the stern upward and out of the water.

Stage 2
The weight of the water inside the hull pulled the bow under. By now the stern was up in the air, causing deck equipment, engines, and internal fixtures to break loose.

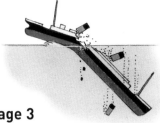

Stage 3
The keel could stand the strain no more and fractured between the third and fourth funnels.

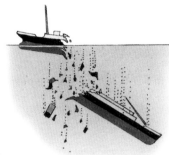

Stage 4
The bow plummeted downward to the seabed. It broke free of the stern section, which floated by itself momentarily before it too sank.

Sliced by ice
It was long thought that the iceberg sliced into the *Titanic*, causing one continuous gash along the hull. Recent sonar images, however, show that the iceberg actually made six narrow holes in the ship's hull.

Hand-clean only
The only way to restore sea-damaged clothes is by hand. With careful brushing and the use of sensitive cleaning materials, the effects of almost 100 years under the sea can slowly be reversed.

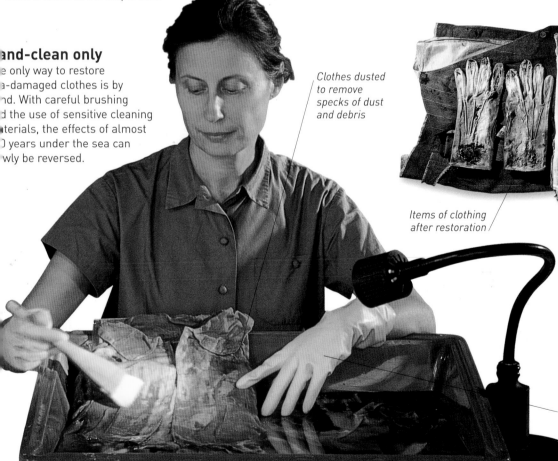

Clothes dusted to remove specks of dust and debris

Items of clothing after restoration

Rubber gloves protect hands against the harmful effects of chemicals

Good as new
Many items of clothing from the wreck were remarkably well preserved, having been stored in trunks or drawers. Clothes recovered include a pair of gloves, a pressed shirt, and a steward's jacket.

Never-ending story

ONCE THEY SAID GOD HIMSELF COULDN'T SINK HER.
NOW THEY SAY NO MAN ON EARTH COULD RAISE HER.

RAISE THE TITANIC

LORD GRADE presents a MARTIN STARGER PRODUCTION
JASON ROBARDS · RICHARD JORDAN · DAVID SELBY · ANNE ARCHER
and ALEC GUINNESS
RAISE THE TITANIC
Produced by WILLIAM FRYE Directed by JERRY JAMESON Screenplay by ADAM KENNEDY
Adaptation by ERIC HUGHES Based on the novel by CLIVE CUSSLER Music by JOHN BARRY

A drop in the ocean
The film *Raise the Titanic* (1980) was a huge failure. It cost $40 million and made so little money that its producer remarked, "It would have been cheaper to lower the Atlantic."

With countless movies, books, musicals, songs, computer games, and websites to its name, the ill-fated *Titanic* is now more famous than ever. Phrases associated with the ship—"and the band played on" and "tip of the iceberg"—have entered the English language, and there can be few people who do not have some knowledge of this fascinating story. The *Titanic* may lie rusting at the bottom of the Atlantic, but interest in the ship—and the magical era to which it belonged—live on.

Memorial edition of the Daily Graphic, April 20, 1912

Daily Mirror, April 16, 1912

Supplement to the Sphere Magazine, April 27, 1912

Sheet music for The Wreck of the Titanic, written by Haydon Augarde

The Deathless Story of the Titanic, *issued by Lloyds Weekly News, 1912*

Sheet music for The Ship That Will Never Return, written by F. V. St. Clair

Silent star
One survivor to prosper from the tragedy was the actress Dorothy Gibson, who escaped in one of the lifeboats. A month after the ship sank, she starred in a silent movie, *Saved from the Titanic*, and went on to have a successful film career.

In pri[nt]
Within days of the disas[ter] newspapers were produc[ed] memorial editions pack[ed] with photographs and artis[ts'] reconstructions. Songwrit[ers] produced mournful son[gs,] postcard companies print[ed] memorial cards, a[nd] publishers produced has[tily] written boo[ks.]

Walter Lord

Walter Lord's book *A Night To Remember* (1955) was based on interviews with more than 60 survivors of the disaster. The book was televised in 1956 and turned into a successful documentary-style film in 1958.

Kenneth More as Second Officer Lightoller

TITANIC...
The greatest sea-drama in living memory
**TOLD AS IT REALLY HAPPENED
TO MAKE THE SCREEN'S
MIGHTIEST MOTION PICTURE**

THE RANK ORGANISATION PRESENTS WITH PRIDE
Kenneth More
A NIGHT TO REMEMBER
FROM THE BOOK BY WALTER LORD · SCREENPLAY BY ERIC AMBLER · PRODUCED BY WILLIAM MacQUITTY · DIRECTED BY ROY BAKER

3-D reconstruction

On a 3-D *Titanic* video game, you can wander around the ship, explore the public rooms and cabins, stand on deck, and relive the ship's final moments.

Titanic musicals

Based on the larger-than-life character of Molly Brown (p. 40), the musical *The Unsinkable Molly Brown* opened in New York in 1960 and was a great success. The musical, *Titanic* (above), staged in 1997, highlighted the great divide between the rich passengers in first class and the poor emigrants in third class.

Kate Winslet and Leonardo DiCaprio star in the film Titanic *(1997)*

The big time

The movie *Titanic*, released in 1997, was one of the most successful films of all time. Directed by James Cameron and starring Kate Winslet and Leonardo DiCaprio, the film won 11 Oscars. Within two years, it had taken 1.8 billion at the box office.

Raise the *Titanic*?

Ever since the ship sank in 1912, plans have been put forward to raise the *Titanic* off the seabed. Suggestions included attaching magnets or bags of helium to the ship's hull. There was even a scheme to fill the ship with table-tennis balls! As the debate over whether to raise the *Titanic* or leave it in peace goes on, the rusting wreck continues to disintegrate.

The *Titanic* lives on

A century after the disaster, people continue to be fascinated by the ship's tragic end. Exhibitions of artifacts tour the world, and a new museum has opened in Belfast. Recent evidence published in 2010 suggests a different twist to the story, but the reality is there will never be a definite answer as to why a brand-new ship should have sunk so quickly.

THE SPHERE

A model of the *Titanic* showing it on the seabed

Seen by millions

Artifacts from the wreck are on display in nine museums in the US and Paris and constantly tour the world. Millions of people visit the exhibitions, which include models of the ship on the seabed.

Robert Hichens

Some people claim that a steering error caused the tragedy. First Officer Murdoch used the old tiller commands to tell Robert Hichens to steer left. Hichens, however, was used to modern commands and turned the wheel so that the ship turned right, straight into the iceberg.

Angular steel walls recall the ship's prow—the front part that cuts through the water

Reviving Belfast

Titanic Belfast (*right*), a major new museum dedicated to the *Titanic*, opened in 2012 in Belfast, where the ship was built. The building sits on ground previously occupied by the Harland and Wolff shipyard. The area is part of a major plan to revive Belfast's economy.

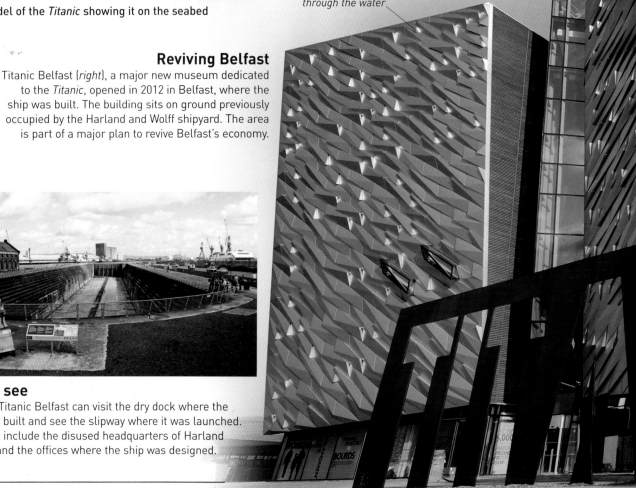

More to see

Visitors to Titanic Belfast can visit the dry dock where the *Titanic* was built and see the slipway where it was launched. Other sites include the disused headquarters of Harland and Wolff and the offices where the ship was designed.

Charles Lightoller

[Se]cond Officer Lightoller had [to g]ive evidence to both the [U]S and British inquiries. [How]ever, he was persuaded [by B]ruce Ismay to mislead [bo]th inquiries because the *Titanic* was inadequately [crewe]d. Lightoller kept quiet [to try] to save everyone's job.

Bruce Ismay

Chairman of the White Star Line, Bruce Ismay, ordered Captain Smith to keep the *Titanic* moving slowly ahead after the collision. This made it sink far quicker than it otherwise would have and led to many unnecessary deaths. As a result of the disaster, his reputation was destroyed and Ismay kept out of the public eye until he died in 1937.

Bruce Ismay giving evidence to the inquiry into the sinking

Louise Patten

Novelist Louise Patten is the granddaughter of Charles Lightoller (above). In 2010, she published a novel *Good as Gold*, in which she used information passed down from her grandfather to claim that a basic steering error was a main cause of the disaster.

Did you know?

AMAZING FACTS

Loading coal at the docks

★ The *Titanic* was carrying 6,598 tons (5,986 metric tons) of coal.

★ Chief Baker Charles Joughin was standing on the stern as the ship sank; he was able just to step into the water. He survived in the freezing ocean for two hours until survivors eventually managed to pull him into Lifeboat 12.

★ Tins of crackers and water were stowed in the lifeboats, but the survivors did not know it.

★ There were at least nine dogs on board ship. Three of the dogs survived.

Harland and Wolff workmen tightening bolts

★ Harland and Wolff employed more than 15,000 workmen to build the *Olympic* and the *Titanic*.

★ Third-class fare on the *Titanic* was just over £7 ($40), including meals. A second-class ticket cost £13 ($65); first-class fare was £86 ($430). Tickets for promenade suites on B deck were £870 ($4,350).

★ Among the goods transported by the *Titanic* were 12 cases of ostrich plumes.

★ Richard Norris Williams refused to have his legs amputated after being rescued from the *Titanic*. He went on to recover fully and won an Olympic gold medal for tennis in 1924.

★ A daily newspaper called the *Atlantic Daily Bulletin* was produced on board.

Richard Norris Williams

Ostrich feather

★ You can smell icebergs before you see them! Minerals give off a distinct smell as the ice melts.

★ There were only two bathtubs on board for more than 700 third-class passengers.

★ There was a small hole in the bottom of each lifeboat, to ensure that water did not collect in the boat while on deck. Lifeboat 5 had reached the water before its hole was blocked.

★ The lights were working on the *Titanic* until two minutes before it sank.

★ There was a 50-phone switchboard on the *Titanic*. The crew, and some first-class passengers, could talk to each other, but it was not possible to speak to people on land.

★ The original plans allowed room for 64 lifeboats. However, the owners and builders of the *Titanic* reduced the number to 16 to provide more space for passengers on the boat deck. They added four lifeboats with collapsible sides.

QUESTIONS AND ANSWERS

Q Why were third-class passengers given a medical check on boarding?

A As emigrants, they were given a medical check to make sure they were healthy to enter America.

Q What are growlers?

A Slabs of ice broken away from icebergs are known as growlers.

Q What were the *Titanic*'s two masts used for?

A A crane on the foremast lifted cars and heavy goods. A ladder inside the foremast led up to the crow's nest. Wires stretched between the two formed part of the wireless communication system.

Q How many lifeboats are there on ships today?

A Modern cruise ships have enough lifeboats for 25 percent more people than are on board.

Q On finding the *Titanic*'s hull, what did explorers see on the foremast?

A After the foremast collapsed across the deck, the crow's nest was seen.

There is no smoke from the fourth funnel

Q What happened to sick people on the *Titanic*?

A There was a hospital with two doctors.

Q Why did the *Titanic* have four funnels?

A The *Titanic*'s owners thought four funnels looked better than three.

Q Why didn't the lookouts use binoculars?

A Lookouts Frederick Fleet and Reginald Lee thought the binoculars were left in Southampton.

Q Why was the *Titanic*'s maiden voyage delayed from March 20 to April 10, 1912?

A When the *Olympic* collided with HMS *Hawke* in September 1911, work was stopped on the *Titanic* to repair the hole in *Olympic*'s side.

The bow of the *Titanic* on the seabed

Record Breakers

⚓ In 1912, the *Olympic* and the *Titanic* were the largest ships in the world, with a length of 882 ft 9 in (269.10 m) and a width of 92 ft 6 in (28 m).

⚓ The *Titanic* was the largest man-made object that had ever been moved.

⚓ The two parlor suites on B deck were the most beautifully decorated staterooms on any ocean liner.

⚓ To build the *Olympic* and the *Titanic*, Harland and Wolff constructed a huge metal framework, called a gantry. It was the largest gantry in the world.

The White Star Line's New Triple-screw Steamers
"OLYMPIC" ☆ "TITANIC"
LARGEST AND FINEST IN THE WORLD

A contemporary postcard comparing the *Titanic* to the world's tallest buildings

Timeline

The building of the RMS *Titanic* and its tragic loss is a story that has fascinated countless people over the last century. This timeline sets out the key points, from the initial idea of the liner, through its design, construction, and launch, to the fatal collision with the iceberg, the sinking, and finally, many decades later, the discovery of the wreck.

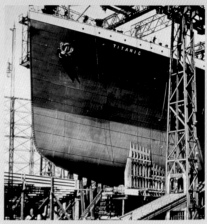
The construction of the *Titanic*

Two of the *Titanic*'s huge propellers

- **SUMMER 1907** Lord Pirrie, chairman of Harland and Wolff, and Bruce Ismay, director of the White Star Line, decide to build three huge, luxurious liners called *Olympic*, *Titanic*, and *Britannic*.

- **MARCH 31, 1909** Construction of the *Titanic* begins.

- **MAY 31, 1911** The *Titanic* is launched.

- **MAY 31, 1912** Fitting is complete and the *Titanic* is ready to sail.

- **APRIL 2, 1912** Tugs pull the *Titanic* out to sea for its sea trials. **8:00 p.m.** The *Titanic* leaves Belfast for Southampton.

- **APRIL 3, 1912** The *Titanic* arrives in Southampton.

- **APRIL 4–10, 1912** Last-minute painting and the fitting of furniture and carpets; the hiring of the crew; loading coal, cargo, and provisions for the trip.

- **WEDNESDAY, APRIL 10, 1912**
6:00 a.m. Crew board *Titanic*.
7:30 a.m. Captain Smith boards.
9:30 a.m Bruce Ismay arrives. He will stay in a parlor suite with a private promenade deck.
9:30–11:30 a.m. Passengers board.
12:00 noon *Titanic* finally sets sail for France, but is slightly delayed by the near collision with the *New York*.

Third-class daily menu

6:35 p.m. *Titanic* drops anchor in Cherbourg harbor. Two small White Star steamships bring passengers, luggage, and mail out to the *Titanic*. **8:10 p.m.** *Titanic* sets off for Ireland.

- **THURSDAY, APRIL 11, 11:30 a.m.** *Titanic* arrives at Queenstown and anchors 2 miles (3 km) offshore.
1:30 p.m. *Titanic* leaves Queenstown and sets sail for New York.

- **FRIDAY, APRIL 12** *Titanic* receives wireless messages of congratulations on the maiden voyage and also warning that there is ice in the sea-lanes. Captain Smith steers farther south.

- **SATURDAY, APRIL 13, 11:00 p.m.** The wireless machine stops working. Jack Phillips and his assistant, Harold Bride, work all night and repair it by 5:00 a.m.

Titanic leaves Queenstown (now known as Cobh)

- **Sunday, April 14, 9:00 a.m.** *Titanic* receives ice warnings from the *Caronia*.
11:40 a.m. Liner *Noordam* reports ice.
1:42 p.m. White Star Liner *Baltic* warns of icebergs and field ice. Captain Smith shows this warning to Bruce Ismay.
1:45 p.m. German liner *Amerika* reports two large icebergs. This message fails to reach Captain Smith.

Harold Bride at work in the radio room

7:30 p.m. Harold Bride overhears an ice warning from the *Californian* and sends it to the bridge.
9:30 p.m. Second Officer Lightoller instructs the lookouts to watch for ice.
9:30 p.m. The *Mesaba* warns of large icebergs. Jack Phillips is busy and does not send the warning to the bridge.

Lifeboats row away as the stern sinks

10:55 p.m. Jack Phillips, exhausted, cuts off the *Californian*'s ice warning.
11:40 p.m. Lookout Frederick Fleet sees the iceberg. First Officer Murdoch gives the order to stop the engines, tells Quartermaster Hichens to turn "hard a'starboard" (left), and closes the doors between the watertight compartments.
11:40 p.m. The *Titanic* hits the iceberg, only 37 seconds after Fleet's warning.
11:41 p.m. Captain Smith instructs Fourth Officer Boxhall to inspect the ship for damage.
11:50 p.m. Thomas Andrews inspects the damaged areas.

- **Monday, April 15, 12:00 midnight** Thomas Andrews tells Captain Smith the ship will sink within 90 minutes.

12:05 a.m. Captain Smith orders the lifeboats to be uncovered.
12:10 a.m. Captain Smith asks Jack Phillips to send out a call for help. The *Olympic*, *Frankfurt*, and *Carpathia* reply.
12:25 a.m. *Carpathia* sets off to help, but is 58 miles (93 km) away.
12:45 a.m. The first lifeboat is lowered.
12:45 a.m. The first distress flare is sent.
About 1:00 a.m. First news reaches the US that the *Titanic* has hit an iceberg.
2:05 a.m. The last lifeboat is lowered.
2:17 a.m. The bow plunges underwater.
2:18 a.m. The *Titanic* breaks into two. The bow section sinks.
2:20 a.m. Two of the collapsible lifeboats wash overboard, one half-flooded, the other upside down.
2:20 a.m. The stern sinks.
4:10 a.m. Survivors from the first lifeboat board the *Carpathia*.
8.10 a.m. Survivors from the last lifeboat board the *Carpathia*.
12:00 p.m. Reports reach New York that the *Titanic* is still afloat and all are safe.
6:16 p.m. Captain Haddock of the *Olympic* confirms that the *Titanic* has sunk.

The Titanic's *propellers rise out of the water*

- **Tuesday, April 16** A list of survivors is posted at the *New York Times* office.

- **Wednesday, April 17** The steamer *Mackay-Bennett* leaves Halifax. It searches the area for nine days and finds 306 bodies. Later, steamers find another 22 bodies.

- **Thursday, April 18** *Carpathia* reaches New York with 705 survivors.

- **April 19–May 25** Inquiry into the disaster by the US Senate.

- **May 2–July 3** British Board of Trade inquiry into the disaster.

- **May 14** Dorothy Gibson, one of the survivors, writes and stars in a silent movie, *Saved from the Titanic*.

Survivors reach the *Carpathia*

- **July 3, 1958** World première of the movie *A Night To Remember*.

- **1960** Opening of the musical *The Unsinkable Molly Brown*.

- **July 1980, June 1981, July 1983** American Jack Grimm leads three attempts to find the wreck.

- **September 1, 1985** Robert Ballard's French/US expedition, with search ship *Knorr* and uncrewed submersible *Argo*, discovers the wreck of the *Titanic*.

- **July 1986** Robert Ballard photographs the wreck in a submarine named *Alvin*.

- **July 1987** A salvaging expedition, with search ship *Nadir* and crewed submersible *Nautile*, starts lifting objects from the wreck. Further expeditions in 1993 and 1994 raise more than 5,000 objects.

Newspaper headlines about the disaster

- **1991** A Soviet/Canadian expedition films the wreck for a documentary called *Titanica*.

- **Dec 18, 1997** The movie *Titanic* opens in the US.

- **April 2003** Première of the film *Ghosts of the Abyss*.

The crewed submersible *Nautile*

Find out more

If the story of the *Titanic* has captured your imagination, there are many ways you can find out more. Exhibitions about the *Titanic*, for instance, often include objects from the wreck. You can learn more about the ship by making a model of it or looking at plans. Watching a film about the *Titanic* will also help bring the liner's tragic journey to life.

Olympic story

By finding out about the *Titanic*'s sister ship, the *Olympic*, you will learn a great deal about the design and style of the *Titanic*.

The grand staircase

Organizers of exhibitions about the *Titanic* try to re-create the atmosphere on board and give an idea of the different experiences of first-class, second-class, and third-class passengers. The ornate grand staircase was one of the most striking parts of the *Titanic*'s first-class accommodation.

USEFUL WEBSITES

- To find out about the *Titanic* Historical Society, see: **www.titanic1.org**
- For all kinds of information about the *Titanic*, go to: **www.titanic-titanic.com**
- To learn about individual passengers and crew members, see: **www.encyclopedia-titanica.org**
- For a transcript of the US Senate and British Board of Trade inquiry, go to: **www.titanicinquiry.org**
- For information on the Titanic Belfast museum, see: **www.titanicbelfast.com**

The Belfast Titanic *memorial was unveiled on June 26, 1920*

Remembering the dead

Many memorials have been dedicated to the people lost on the *Titanic*. In Southampton, UK, there are separate memorials to the engineers, firemen, musicians, and postmen who worked on the *Titanic*. In Belfast, Northern Ireland, there is a memorial for the 22 Ulstermen who died in the disaster.

A *Titanic* model

Constructing a model of the *Titanic* will help you understand its incredible size. You will find out where the lifeboats were kept and discover how frightening it was for the people in the lifeboats to be lowered 60 ft (18 m) down to the water.

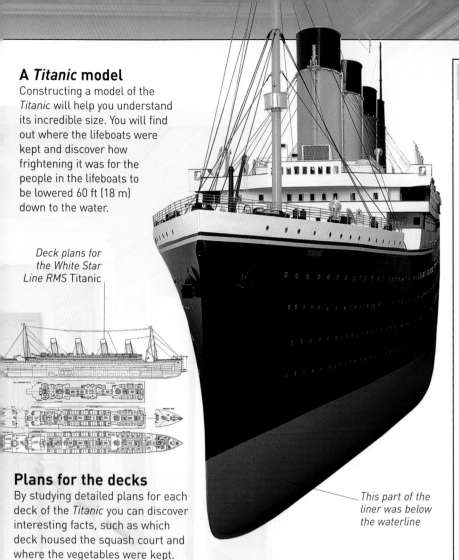

Deck plans for the White Star Line RMS *Titanic*

Plans for the decks

By studying detailed plans for each deck of the *Titanic* you can discover interesting facts, such as which deck housed the squash court and where the vegetables were kept.

This part of the liner was below the waterline

Ghosts of the Abyss

If you want to know more about the *Titanic* wreck, watch the 2003 film *Ghosts of the Abyss* by James Cameron, director of *Titanic*. Using digital 3-D technology, the movie takes you on an amazing expedition to the seabed for a trip around the wreck.

PLACES TO VISIT

THE MARINER'S MUSEUM
NEWPORT NEWS, VIRGINIA
• The displays of oceangoing commercial steamships, in the Great Hall of Steam Gallery, include an exhibit on the *Titanic*.

THE MARITIME MUSEUM
FALL RIVER, MASSACHUSETTS
• The museum's collection includes photographs, the account of a *Titanic* survivor, a video of the underwater discovery, and the centerpiece, a 28-ft (2.5-m) model of the RMS *Titanic*.

THE TITANIC MEMORIAL LIGHTHOUSE
NEW YORK, NEW YORK
• The lighthouse stands 60 ft (18.3 m) at the entrance of the South Street Seaport in Manhattan. It holds a light that stands as a tribute to the people who died on the *Titanic*. The Memorial Light originally stood at the old Seaman's Church Institute, where it signaled to ships in the harbor.

THE TITANIC MUSEUM
INDIAN ORCHARD, MASSACHUSETTS
• Edward S. Kamuda founded this private museum in 1963 for the survivors of the ship. It contains a unique collection of personal items from survivors, such as letters, postcards, and menus.

MARITIME MUSEUM OF THE ATLANTIC
HALIFAX, CANADA
• The exhibition features artifacts pulled from the water within weeks of the tragedy, including a deckchair and part of the grand staircase, and it traces the creation of this "floating palace."

Medal given to the crew of the *Carpathia*

Finding salvage

Here a robotic arm is lifting a masthead lamp from the wreck site. Many of the items found at the site feature in touring exhibitions. It is worth seeking out these collections to build a more complete picture of life on board the *Titanic*.

Glossary

AFT At the rear of a ship.

AFT DECK An open deck at the back of the ship for use by third-class passengers.

BERTH A cabin bed or bunk.

BOAT DECK The deck on which the lifeboats are stored.

BOILER A container that heats water to supply steam or heat.

BOW The front part of the ship.

BRIDGE The control center of the ship.

BULKHEAD The wall in the hold of a ship that can create a watertight compartment.

CABIN An office or living room on a ship.

CLIPPER SHIP A fast sailing ship.

COLLAPSIBLE A lifeboat with canvas sides that collapse for easy storage.

CQD An international Morse code distress call; it was later replaced by SOS.

CREW The people who run a ship. There were 898 on the *Titanic*'s crew list: 875 men and 23 women.

A. M. Carlisle, designer of the *Titanic*, at the British investigation

CROW'S NEST A lookout platform high on a ship's mast. On the *Titanic*, the crow's nest was 90 ft (27 m) above the water.

DAVIT A cranelike device fitted with pulleys and ropes and used to lower lifeboats.

DRY DOCK A dock that can be pumped dry for work on the bottom of a ship.

ENGINEER A person who helps run the engines and machines.

ENSIGN A flag distinguishing a country or company.

FIREMAN Someone who loads coal into the ship's boilers.

FITTING OUT Installing the decks, machinery, and other equipment inside the empty hull.

FUNNEL A chimney through which smoke from the engines escapes.

FURNACES An enclosed chamber in which coal burns to produce heat.

GANGWAY A passageway into a ship.

The 1958 film *A Night To Remember*

GENERAL ROOM A public room like a lounge for the third-class passengers.

GRAND STAIRCASE The staircase connecting the first-class dining salon with the first-class promenade deck.

GREASER A person who attends to a ship's engines.

A washbasin from the wreck

HOLD The space for storing cargo.

HULL The main body of a ship.

ICEFIELD A large area of ice in the sea.

INSPECTION CARD Carried by emigrants, the card states the person's name, former country of residence, port of departure, and vessel for the journey.

KEEL The bottom structure that runs the length of a ship in the very center and to which the frames fasten.

LINER A large passenger ship that sails fixed routes ("lines").

LOOKOUTS The *Titanic* had six lookouts. Working in pairs they kept watch for other ships or obstacles ahead from the crow's nest on the foremast.

A reconstruction of the first-class verandah café on the *Titanic*

LOWER DECK This is the deck above the orlop deck. On the *Titanic* it was just above the waterline.

MAIDEN VOYAGE A ship's first journey.

MORSE CODE A telegraph code used to send messages. A system of dots and dashes represents letters and numbers.

ORLOP DECK The lowest deck.

PASSAGEWAY A walkway between cabins or other rooms.

POOP DECK A raised deck at the stern of a ship.

PORT The left-hand side of a ship.

PORTHOLE A small, usually round, window in the side of a ship. There were about 2,000 portholes and windows on the *Titanic*.

PROMENADE DECK An upper deck where people could take a walk.

PROPELLERS Three large propellers, driven by the engine, moved the *Titanic*.

QUARTERMASTER A junior officer who was responsible for navigation.

READING ROOM A spacious, quiet room used by for reading and writing.

RIVETS A short metal pin used to fasten things together.

ROYAL MAIL SHIP (RMS) A ship with a contract to carry mail from one place to another. The *Titanic* was carrying 3,364 sacks of mail.

RUDDER A vertical fin at the back of a ship used for steering.

SALON A large, public room on a ship. The first-class dining salon was the largest room on the *Titanic*. It could seat 550 people.

SEA TRIALS Tests conducted at sea on a new ship to make sure the engines and steering are working well.

SHIPPING LINE A company that owns and runs passenger or freight ships.

SISTER SHIP One that is the same class and belongs to the same line.

SOS A Morse code distress call. The *Titanic* was one of the first ships to use this code.

STARBOARD The right-hand side of a ship.

STATEROOM A first-class private cabin.

STEAM TURBINE A machine that takes the energy of steam and turns it into the movement of a propeller.

STEERAGE The cheapest accommodation on a ship.

STERN The rear part of a ship.

STOKER A person who looks after the furnaces on a steamship.

SUBMERSIBLE A submarine designed and equipped to carry out work deep on the seabed.

A doll rescued from the *Titanic*

One of *Titanic*'s lifeboats

TRIMMER A person who wheels coal to the boilers and ensures that the remaining fuel is evenly distributed so that the ship is balanced.

TURKISH BATH A steam bath.

WHEELHOUSE The enclosed structure on the bridge of a ship where officers steer the vessel.

WIRELESS OPERATORS The two people, employed by Marconi, who sent Morse code telegraph messages.

The *Titanic*'s bow on the seabed

Index

Acknowledgments

Dorling Kindersley would like to thank:
Richard Chasemore for *Titanic* illustration (pp. 12–16)
Illustrators: John Woodcock, Hans Jenssen
Indexer: Chris Bernstein
Researcher: Robert Graham
Editorial assistance: Carey Scott

For this edition, the publisher would also like to thank: Hazel Beynon for text editing and Carron Brown for proofreading.

The publisher would like to thank the following for their kind permission to reproduce their photographs:
(Key: a-above; b-below/bottom; c-center; f-far; l-left; r-right; t-top)

Alamy Images: Dinodia Photo Library 68–69 bckgrd; Elizabeth Leyden 62bl; INTERFOTO / Cinema 49bl; Vintage Image 49ca; PF-(bygone) 50cr; **AKG London:** 19br; 23 tr, 37bl, 40– 41, 44b; **Howard Barlow:** 67br; **Bridgeman Art Library, London / New York:** © Browne, Father Frank (1880–1960) / Father Browne SJ Collection 48b; Harley Crossley 38–39; V & A Museum, London 8tr; **British Sailors' Society:** 4r, 34c; **Christie's Images Ltd. 1999:** 43tl; **Colorific:** 19tl, 67cr; P; Landmann / Arenok 4br, 5tr, 5br, 5tl, 6br, 6tl, 6tr, 19cr, 29tl, 30bl, 66br, 66tr, 67bl; RMS Titanic / Arenok 66cl; **Corbis UK Ltd.:** 9br, 11br, 18tr, 25tr, 34bl, 38l, 39tc, 47c, 66br, 71tr, 66–67, 70bl, 70br, 67tl, 12bl, 68cl; Bertrand Rieger / Hemis 62–63b; Bettmann 11tr, 51b, 63tr, 70bl; Bettmann / UPI 42tl, 70bl; The Mariners Museum, Virginia 17tr, 71cl; Christie's Images 70tl; Hulton–Deutsch Collection 50tl, 70tr; Ma Jianguo 51cla; Polak Matthew 71bl; Splash News 49tl; Geray Sweeney 70bl; Ralph White 67br, 68tr, 71b; **Cyberflix:** 21tr, 71tr; **DK Images:** Judith Miller and Cobwebs of Southampton 70tr; Southampton City Cultural Services 71clb; **E.T. Archive:** Denis Cochrane Collection 6cr, 66tl; **Frank Spooner Pictures:** 36bl, 71br; Jahiel/ Liaison/ Gamma, 26tr, 71bl, 66bc; Liaison/ Gamma 40t; **Getty Images:** AFP PHOTO / JOEL SAGET 62cla; LatitudeStock—Allan Hartley 4l; English School / The Bridgeman Art Library 51cl; **Harland & Wolff Photographic Collection:** 10–11, 11cr, 11tl, 12tr, 12br, 13tl, 22br, 29br; **Hulton Getty:** 13br, 18bl, 28cl, 28c, 35tr, 38bl, 41tl, 43tr, 45tr, 46br, 67bl, 70r, 71l; **Illustrated London News Library:** 37br, 70b; **The Irish Picture Library:** © Father S. J. Brown Collection 20br; **John Frost Newspapers:** 47bl, 47tr; **Kobal Collection:** 20th C; Fox / Paramount 32l; Merie W. Wallace 24c; **Courtesy of James & Felicia Kreuzer:** 32cl; **Stanley Lehrer:** 20cr, 23cr, 45br; **Paul Louden-Brown** Collection: 10l, 27tr, 66cl; **Joe Low:** 24tl, 42–43; **Joan Marcus:** 71tr; **Courtesy of The Mariner's Museum, Newport News VA:** 36tr, 38tr, 43cr, 45tl; Photographed by Learning Resources Technology, courtesy of the Maritime Museum of the Atlantic, Halifax, Nova Scotia, Canada: 37bc; **Library Of Congress, Washington, D.C.:** 48tr; **Mary Evans Picture Library:** 6bl, 9bc, 15tr, 23tl, 24–25, 25cl, 26–27, 26tl, 26cc, 27cr, 32bl, 34–35, 37tl, 41tr, 42, 44r, 45bl, 66cl, 67tl, 67tr; **National Maritime Museum, London:** 5bl, 9tr, 13tr, 20cr, 21bl, 23br, 29cl, 35br, 39cr, 70tl, 70–71; **National Museums and Galleries of Northern Ireland, Ulster Folk and Transport Museum:** 13bl; **National Museums and Galleries on Merseyside:** 4, 23c, 71tc; **Onslow's Titanic Picture Library:** 7, 14tl, 19cl, 21br, 21tl, 27br, 28b, 29bl, 30cl, 32br, 67cr; **The Picture Desk:** The Art Archive / Ocean Memorabilia Collection 69cl, 69tl, 71tr; **Photo SCALA, Florence:** English Library board / Robana 62tr; **Photoshot:** UPPA 63tl; **Popperfoto:** 18–19, 30tl, 71b; Onslow's 28tr, 70r; **Quadrant Picture Library:** Mike Nicholson 71cr; **Rex Features:** 10tr, 34tl, 34tr, 36br, 40l, 63br, 71bl; Charles Sachs 19tr; Mike Lawn 51tl; Nils Jorgansen 6cl, 16t; Sipa 44tl; Sipa (Cork Examiner) 31tl, Peter Brooker 70tr, 70–71 bckgrd; **Ronald Grant Archive:** 70tl, 71tl; **Science & Society Picture Library:** 8b, 8cr; **Southampton City Cultural Services:** 21c, 23bl, 47br, 69tr, 69c; **Still Pictures:** B & C Alexander 22cl; Vincent Bretagnolle 33b; **Sygma / RMS Titanic Inc.:** 71tl, 71cra, Bourseiller 28bl; Sotheby's 66cr; **The Titanic Historical Society Collection:** 4tr, 26bl, 27tl, 30–31b, 31cl, 33tl, 41cr, 46tl; Courtesy Mrs Ruth Becker Blanchard 44cl; Goldsmith 31tr; Ken Marschall 67c; **Courtesy of © "Titanic Survivor" by Violet Jessop** edited by John Maxtone-Graham—Sheridan House Inc.—1997: 67tr;Topham Picturepoint: 18tr, 20bl, 22bl, 29tr, 33tr, 35tc, 36tl, 39tl, 46c, 67br; Buena Vista Pictures 71cbc; PressNet 68cc; UPPA 11tl, 36tl, 49tl; **TopFoto.co.uk:** The Granger Collection 48cr; 49cl; 50cl; 50c; 50b **Vintage Magazine Company Ltd.:** 31cr; **Louis Vuitton, Paris:** 24cl; **Stuart Williamson:** 67tl, 71br

All other images
© Dorling Kindersley
For further information see: **www.dkimages.com**